BACKYARDS
ARE
FOR
THE BIRDS

BACKYARDS
ARE
FOR
THE BIRDS

Creating a Bird-friendly Environment Outside Your Window

Edward R. Ricciuti

Illustrations by John Lane

AVON BOOKS ◆ NEW YORK

AVON BOOKS
A division of
The Hearst Corporation
1350 Avenue of the Americas
New York, New York 10019

Copyright © 1998 by Edward R. Ricciuti
Interior Illustrations copyright © 1998 by John Lane
Interior back cover author photograph by Wildlife Conservation Society,
    headquartered at the Bronx Zoo
Interior design by Stanley S. Drate/Folio Graphics Co. Inc.
Published by arrangement with the author
Visit our website at **http://www.AvonBooks.com**
ISBN: 0-380-79268-0

Library of Congress Cataloging in Publication Data

Ricciuti, Edward R.
    Backyards are for the birds : creating a bird-friendly environment
outside your window / by Edward R. Ricciuti.
        p. cm.
    1. Bird attracting.   I. Title.
    QL676.5.R535   1998   97-34845
    639.9′78′097—DC21   CIP

First Avon Books Trade Printing: April 1998

AVON TRADEMARK REG. U.S. PAT. OFF. AND IN OTHER COUNTRIES, MARCA REGISTRADA, HECHO EN U.S.A.

Printed in the U.S.A.

OPM   10 9 8 7 6 5 4 3 2 1

To my Thursday night friends,
who know their birds

CONTENTS

Chapter 1

FATAL ATTRACTION   1

Here is a look at the reciprocal attraction between birds and
humans. You'll learn about the history of birding in America
and find out the benefits that accrue from making your yard a
better place for birds to live.

Chapter 2

THE BIRDS   8

Explore the biology of birds, from their dinosaur origins to the
way their feathers help them fly. Find out how the Connecticut
warbler got its name, even though it hardly ever visits that
state. Learn why some birds migrate and what
makes a "perching bird."

Chapter 3

WHY BIRDS BEHAVE THE WAY THEY DO   24

Take a peek inside a bird's brain and see how it works. Here's why and how birds defend their turf. If woodpeckers sometimes use your house for a sounding board, learn why they do it. After reading this chapter, you will know more about what's behind the behavior of birds in your backyard.

Chapter 4

BACKYARD BIRDING BASICS   35

Even if you are an expert birder, you'll find tips in this chapter that will make you better. If you're just starting out, this chapter is a must. Learn how to invest wisely in binoculars, how to choose a good field guide, how to get started feeding the birds, and much more.

Chapter 5

BEWILDERED BY BIRDSEED?   49

This chapter will save you money. It will teach you the plain facts about birdseed, how to pick the right kind of seed for your needs, and how to avoid buying seed that will make birds turn up their beaks.

Chapter 6

FEEDER FRENZY   57

With so many different models and makes of bird feeders on the market, it can be difficult to figure out which is best for your yard. This chapter helps you sort out the confusion. You'll

get tips on buying feeders—and making them, too. And once
you have a feeder, you'll learn how to match it
with the right seed.

Chapter 7

GIVE A POOR BIRD A HOME   68

Birdhouses are more properly called "nest boxes." By either
name, they can be used to attract several types of birds to your
yard, including some species that do not utilize feeding
stations. Here's the scoop on nest boxes for various species
and where to put them.

Chapter 8

NEAT AND NATURAL WAYS
TO ATTRACT BIRDS   80

Make your yard a bird sanctuary. It doesn't have to be difficult.
Here's a chapter outlining several ways you can turn your yard
into a habitat that will entice birds to settle in. Learn about
different plants that attract birds and where to put them. Find
out how a bowl of gravel, a dead tree, or a pile of brush can be
alluring to birds. In short, bring nature back to your backyard.

Chapter 9

BIRD BUTCHERS AND
BACKYARD BANDITS   95

Hawks, raccoons, cats, and squirrels are among the predators
and pests that often drive backyard birders crazy. Here is an
inside look at some of these creatures and how to cope—or try
to cope—with their depredations.

Contents

Chapter 10

TWO DOZEN EXCELLENT
BACKYARD BIRDS

What are the best backyard birds? Here, you'll find profiles of
twenty-four birds that make the author's list. See if you agree.

ACKNOWLEDGMENTS

Rob Braunfield for his helpfulness and courtesy

Donald Bruning Ph.D., Chairman and Curator of Ornithology, Wildlife Conservation Society, for reading the manuscript

Miley Bull, Connecticut Audubon Society, for reading the manuscript

James D'Elia, General Manager, Sports and Recreational Optics, Nikon Inc., for assistance on optics

John Lane for his dedication to his illustrations that accompany the text and for his overall help on this book

INTRODUCTION

The Birds of Killingworth

An unofficial symbol of Killingworth, Connecticut, the small community that counts me among its five thousand odd residents, is a perching songbird. Many local drivers have affixed metal plates with the town's name and a silhouette of the bird to the fronts of their vehicles. This emblem signifies the town's pride generated by the fact that "The Birds of Killingworth" is one of the poems in Henry Wadsworth Longfellow's *Tales of a Wayside Inn*. Longfellow was a resident of Killingworth for a time and, according to local tradition, lived in a building, known as the "old parsonage," across from the market where my wife works.

"The Birds of Killingworth" is an example of textbook environmental writing that still rings true. It vividly describes how humans can bring down calamity upon themselves by tampering with ecological checks and balances—by disturbing Mother Nature's house, in effect. Longfellow tells the story of how Killingworth's farmers, aroused by the depredations of songbirds upon their crops, took their shotguns off their walls and eliminated the offending birds down to the last robin and sparrow. He eloquently describes the consequences of the farmers' rash actions. Bereft of birds, and their color and song, the town became a sad, sterile place. Worse yet, once the birds were gone, the bugs descended on Killingworth like street gangs working the pavement when the cops are out on strike.

Unleashed, without birds to prey upon them, the insects did far more damage to the harvest than the birds could ever have accomplished. The farmers finally came to their senses and hung up their guns, but the damage had been done. It was bye, bye birdie, apparently for good. As a last resort, the town fathers opted for a measure now frequently used by wildlife managers to restore creatures to habitats from which they have been extirpated: reintroduction. Birds were gathered elsewhere in the countryside, placed in wicker cages, and then released in Killingworth. The birds adapted well to their new home and, wrote Longfellow,

> *Their songs burst forth in joyous overflow,*
> *And a new heaven bent over a new earth*
> *Amid the sunny farms of Killingworth.*

Obviously, when the farmers of Killingworth sowed their seed, they had no intention of drawing birds to their fields. But they did, anyhow, and the result was bad news for the birds. On the other side of the coin, since time immemorial people have devoted considerable energies to devising ways to attract birds, with equally dire results for the birds. At least 4,000 years ago, for example, Native American hunters were using decoys made of feathers and plant fibers to draw ducks within projectile or net range. The Indians, of course, did not call these devices "decoys." The word has its roots in an old Dutch term, *de koi,* which means "the cage," and refers to elaborate mazes of cultivated vegetation long utilized by Europeans to channel birds into hidden traps and nets.

Nowadays, people continue to hatch schemes and create gadgets that will attract birds—but for a purpose far different from plucking them and popping them into the pot.

Zillions of Americans set out feeders, water, plantings, and other attractants that will entice birds to their backyards—front yards and windows, too, for that matter—for a visit or, better yet, to take up residence. It's part of the overall birding craze that has swept the country and shows no signs of abating. For me, the birds that live at least part of their lives on my Killingworth property are a joy. They enliven my yard and my life. Making my land friendly for them is a pursuit that is certainly to their benefit—and, perhaps even more so, to mine.

1

FATAL ATTRACTION

Birding—watching and studying birds—is not a new pursuit in the United States. Both professional and amateur naturalists have been spying on birds since the beginning of the republic. The early American birders worked in relative obscurity, but during the first half of the nineteenth century, John James Audubon, famed naturalist, writer, and painter, became a birding superstar. One of Audubon's favorite "avian observation devices," by the way, was the fowling piece. In order to study and paint different species of birds, he had to see them up close, really close. Figuring that a bird in the hand was much easier to examine than two in the bush, Audubon had no qualms about blasting them out of the air or off the branches—for scientific purposes, of course.

The National Pastime

Although Audubon tweaked popular interest in birds, the general public still tended to look upon hard-core birders as bluestockings. As far as the general public was concerned, birders needed to get a life. Meanwhile, however, new birding recruits were steadily, if quietly, joining the ranks. Many of the enlistees mustered in after reading the model for today's ornithological field books, Roger Tory Peterson's *A Field Guide to the Birds*, first published in 1934 and reissued repeatedly since then. Peterson was the Audubon of the twentieth century—and more. With his paintings and prose, he popularized birding at a grassroots level. Even so, it took decades before the general populace decided that bird-watching was not inherently nerdy. I know that from experience. At the beginning of the 1950s, during my adolescence, I first headed into the woods with binoculars and notebook. My uninspired cronies took heed of this odd behavior and tittered. Still, they weren't surprised. What else could they expect from a guy who had flopped as a stickball player? Today, however, even real men boast of their ability to distinguish between downy and hairy woodpeckers. The nation's passion for birding blossomed as environmental awareness began to spread during the 1960s. Watching and enjoying the birds have become the real deal for myriads of people. And birders have never looked back.

The cadre of birders has swelled to an immense army. In 1958, famed ornithologists Allan and Helen Cruikshank noted in one of their books that a million Americans were engaged in birding. By the 1990s, a study commissioned by the United States Fish and Wildlife Service revealed approximately 65 million Americans had at least given birding a try—and 41 million of them bought birdseed. Bird-watching now ranks as the nation's second most popular hobby after gardening. Many people pursue both hobbies in tandem by cultivating plantings that are beneficial to birds.

All in all, myriads of Americans reach deep into their pockets to pay for their addiction to birds. We spend more on birding than on sporting events such as football, basketball, and baseball combined, so a case can be made that birding is our new national pastime. Faced with the choice, some truly passionate bird lovers probably would spend their last cent on food for the birds rather than on themselves. Just as the enticements of Killingworth's fields proved lethal to the birds that succumbed to it, the attraction that birds have for people who are hooked on them can also be fatal—to the family budget. Still, the joys of birding are well worth it—as long as you don't go overboard with your expenditures. Shop around. Not all the birdseed on the shelf works as well as advertised, whatever the price. Figure out whether you want to spend close to $100 on a bird feeder that may outlast you or make one out of a plastic soda bottle that will have to be replaced on occasion. Above all, remember that while you can spend thousands of dollars on trips to exotic bird-watching destinations, some of the true wonders of the avian world are right at home, in your backyard—or even at your apartment window, if you lack grassy space.

Benefits for Both

The relationship between birds and the people who feed them is splendidly symbiotic. The birds benefit from a handy and sustained source of the essentials they need for survival. When natural food is in short supply, many birds may be able to thwart the Grim Reaper because of backyard handouts, although a recent study suggests that feeders are mainly a supplementary food source. There is evidence, moreover, that over many decades the ranges of certain species of birds, like cardinals and tufted titmice, have edged northward at least partly because food is readily available at feeding stations during the winter.

Although their reciprocity is unintentional, birds repay backyard kindnesses in spades. If you are stressed out, instead of visiting a shrink or popping a pill, try watching a company of birds flitting about a feeder. The kaleidoscope of color and motion, different shapes and sizes, and intriguing patterns of behavior will grab your attention and help you forget your troubles.

The pleasures of having birds around the yard can be spectacular or subtle. One morning, while sitting in my upstairs study, I looked out the window and noticed a great blue heron standing in the small pond that borders my backyard lawn. After failing to catch a frog, the heron spread its great wings—this species has a seventy-inch wingspan—and rose into the air. It made a half circle around the yard, then headed for my house, coming so close to where I sat that one of its wing tips passed under the sloping eave of the roof within a foot or so of the window. I have seen wildlife spectacles on five of the seven continents, but this one right in my backyard rates with the best. As for little pleasures, they abound—like the tapping sounds that tell me a titmouse is trying to open a sunflower seed at the kitchen window feeder; the surprisingly loud buzzing of a hummingbird as it makes for bee balm in flower; and the bluebirds that materialize around my untended field, livening up a drab winter's day.

Young children readily respond to the color and movement of birds and quickly learn to enjoy tending to their
needs. Kids can be introduced to nature and taught to appreciate it via a bird-feeding station. A parent can teach
a child heaps about the natural world by explaining the
differences among the various types of birds and their behaviors. Children enjoy filling feeders, just as they enjoy
placing a pinch of fish food in an aquarium, and as they
learn to tend a feeder on a regular basis, they can develop
a sense of responsibility.

At the other end of the age spectrum, feeding birds is a
natural for the elderly, especially those whose movements

are restricted. By placing a feeder outside the window—some aged people may need help putting up the feeder and maintaining it—the elderly can bring nature to them when they can no longer go out and seek it.

Another Benefit from Birds

If you garden, having birds around the yard can be a big plus—as long as you shield your berry crop from their hungry attentions. Many species of birds feast on insects that graze on your vegetable and flower plants. Along with fruits and berries, orioles will feed on bugs, grasshoppers, and beetles. The varied thrush consumes caterpillars, while the red-winged blackbird devours noxious cankerworms, snails that spread their goo on your lettuce, weevils, caterpillars, and grubs. Many birds change their feeding habits according to the season. During the winter, chickadees feed primarily on seeds and berries as well as whatever invertebrates they can find. Naturally, insects are difficult to come by during that time of year. During summer, however, when insects abound and your plants are growing, chickadees make the most of it and switch mostly to animal material, much of which is in the form of caterpillars.

My Yard or Your Yard

Granted, I have tons of stuff in my yard that attracts birds, some of which results from my own efforts. However, I have not always lived in country settings where birds abound, but I have always brought in the birds. Give birds what they want and need, and they will come to you, even in the concrete heart of the city. That's a given.

Admittedly, it takes some cash and a bit of effort to tempt birds to your landholdings. But for millions of us, the time and money are well spent. If, however, you still want birds in your yard but don't want to make the effort, try plastic flamingos.

2

THE BIRDS

Dinosaurs in the Backyard

Imagine looking out the window and seeing a bunch of dinosaurs milling around your bird feeder. According to prevailing scientific wisdom, you don't have to imagine it, because birds are direct descendants of dinosaurs, perhaps even dinosaurs in the flesh. The dinosaur-bird connection was propounded over a century ago, then fell out of grace, only to be resurrected in the past few decades. That is typical of the way scientists regularly rewrite their gospel. One day's truth can be heresy the next, but eventually be reinstated as dogma.

In 1861, when the first fossil of the earliest-known bird, *Archaeopteryx,* was discovered, scientists went into a tizzy. Here was a bird—admittedly an ugly one—that lived about 150 million years in the past, a contemporary of the Jurassic dinosaurs. As if that were not enough to set the scientific world buzzing, *Archaeopteryx* shared many skeletal features with certain dinosaurs. These reptiles soon came to be described as "birdlike dinosaurs." Scientists could also have called *Archaeopteryx* a "dinosaurlike bird," but they didn't. A subsequent *Archaeopteryx* fossil, plus fossils of other primitive birds, revealed jaws containing socketed teeth similar to those of crocodiles—and of dinosaurs. Top paleontologists in the United States and Europe took note of this fact and championed the concept that dinosaurs were the ancestors of modern birds.

During the 1920s, however, scientists shifted gear when ornithologist Gerhard Heilmann pointed out certain inconsistencies in bone structure between birds and various birdlike dinosaurs. He proposed that although birds were related to dinosaurs, it was not by descent but due to the fact that both had a common ancestor. Almost to a researcher, scientists accepted his proposal as a dandy idea and downgraded dinosaurs from the progenitors of birds to their distant cousins.

Scientists changed their tune once again during the 1960s. Dr. John Ostrom of Yale University noted that there were so many skeletal similarities between *Archaeopteryx* and the man-sized, predatory dinosaur *Deinonychus* that the affinities between the two could not be denied. Moreover, the body structure of *Deinonychus* indicated that, like birds, it had a high-powered metabolism; there are even suggestions that it was feathered. The dinosaur connection came back into favor and has gained such acceptance that some dinosaur groupies now gleefully refer to birds as "feathered dinosaurs."

Bundles of Energy

A high-octane metabolism is necessary to provide the copious energy a bird needs for powered flight. A bird literally is a bundle of energy, with a normal body temperature that would fry a human—more than 110 degrees Fahrenheit in some species. Stoking the internal furnace that maintains such high body heat takes plenty of fuel, especially in cold weather. Don't believe the old saying about "eating like a bird." It is pure bunk. Birds stuff themselves at every chance; some songbirds consume a third of their weight in food per day. Birds seem to sense when they need to fill their tanks with fuel. I do not need a barometer to know that atmospheric pressure is going to drop. When a low-pressure system is on the way, juncos, chickadees, titmice, and a bevy of other birds swarm around my feeders and pack away seed with extreme urgency.

To keep the cells of its body supplied with the food and oxygen needed to produce energy, the four-chambered heart of a bird pumps blood at a spectacular rate. By way of comparison, the human heart beats about 70 times a minute, although perhaps a bit faster when someone is angry, frightened, or love struck. A crow's heart rate is more than eight times as fast, and, in a mere second, the tiny hearts of some hummingbirds beat more than 160 times.

Feathers, which are believed to have evolved from reptilian scales, go hand in hand with a high-speed metabolism. They insulate against the cold and dampness, preventing the loss of body heat, enabling birds to be miserly about energy expenditure. When a bird fluffs its feathers on a cold day, it is trapping a layer of air between its inner and outer coats, further adding to its insulation. During warm weather, a bird's feathers may look messy, as if it has not been taking proper care of them. This is not due to a

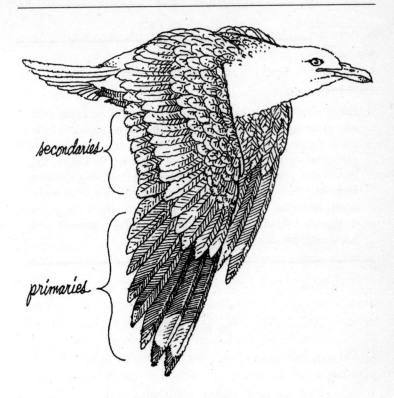

secondaries

primaries

lack of good grooming; the bird has ruffled its plumage so that heat can more readily escape from its body.

Birds actually have good grooming habits. When not eating or sleeping, they are likely to be preening their feathers, a process that involves cleaning them with their bills and then oiling them with a secretion taken from a gland on their rumps. Preen oil spreads more easily when feathers are damp, so bathing not only cleanses a bird with water but helps it condition its plumage. A backyard birdbath, therefore, attracts both birds that are thirsty and those in need of a bath.

Feather Power

Large wing feathers called "primaries" help a bird stay aloft
and move through the air. During the downward beat of the
wing, the primaries flatten out and overlap, creating a contin-
uous surface that generates lift. As the wing descends, the
tips of the primaries twirl, like propellers, driving the bird
forward. When the bird raises its wings, the primaries move
apart, allowing air to pass through them, which decreases
resistance. Meanwhile, the wing tips press upward and
backward, providing additional propulsion.

The Big Three

Obviously, birds need both food and water to survive. They
also need cover, which in a broad sense means places in
which a bird can take shelter, roost, and nest. Cover usually
is provided by vegetation such as trees and shrubs, but not
always. Structures built by humans have profited some
birds that seem especially innovative. Eastern phoebes and
barn swallows, adapted to nesting on cliffs and in rocky
ravines in nature, now more often than not place their
nests under the eaves and on the rafters of buildings. I
haven't used the lamp over my front door during the spring
and summer in years because a pair of house finches regularly nests there. Of course, myriad birds readily use nesting
and roosting boxes. Offering birds the big three essentials
for survival is a surefire way to attract them and keep them
around.

World Citizens

Birds constitute the class of vertebrates called Aves, Latin for—surprise—"with feathers." They inhabit every continent, which is more than can be said for amphibians, reptiles, and land mammals, and they have found their way to

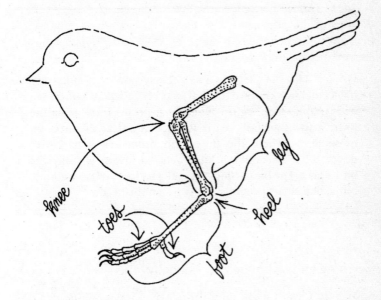

the most remote of oceanic islands. All told, there are about 8,600 species of living birds, about 700 of which can be found at one time of year or another in the United States and Canada. Taxonomists—scientists who make a living classifying animals according to their biological affinities and differences—have divided birds into 28 major groups, or orders. The largest of these by far, including about 6,000 species, is the group known as the perching birds, a name bestowed upon them because their toes are superbly adapted to locking onto branches. Tendons in the legs and feet of perching birds extend all the way down to the tips of their toes. When a perching bird bends its legs and grabs a branch, the tendons tighten, flexing the toes and locking them with a viselike grip.

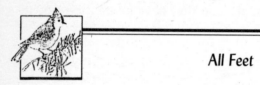

All Feet

When is a leg not a leg but a foot? Even some "authoritative" books on birds confuse the real facts about where a bird's leg ends and its foot begins. What most people think of as the lower part of a bird's leg is its foot. A chicken's knee, for example, is where the thigh and drumstick join. Lower down, what looks like a knee bent backward is really the bird's heel. The bird's "foot" is really its toes. When walking, birds, like smart people, are always on their toes.

Most birds that congregate at backyard feeders are perching birds, although occasionally others, such as woodpeckers, may turn up as well. The name "perching birds" is something of a misnomer because many other kinds of birds also perch, although they lack those special tendons. Perching birds also are known, generically, as "songbirds," another name that is misleading. because not all of them sing melodiously and some don't sing at all. For example, crows are perching birds, but only someone with a tin ear might consider them songsters. Their vocalizations, moreover, are not actually songs but calls.

Geography, surrounding habitat, and season determine the kinds of birds you are likely to see in your backyard.

Some species can handle only very specific environments but, within appropriate habitats, can be quite common. Wile E. Coyote's nemesis, the roadrunner—actually, a big, ground-dwelling cuckoo—lives only in scrubby areas of the arid Southwest. It is relatively abundant in that region and not an uncommon sight in the backyard. In many cases, closely related species have each staked out a different part of the continent. As its name implies, the eastern bluebird lives mostly east of the Great Plains, while the look-alike western bluebird takes over to the west. There are other birds that can tolerate a wide range of living conditions. The American robin is a prime example. Name a North American habitat except tundra or desert and robins are probably hunting worms there. Robins live from coast to coast and during the summer can be found as far north as Alaska, although when winter's chill approaches they abandon the northern portion of their range for milder climes.

See You Next Spring—Or Fall

Seasonal migrations cause the backyard bird scene to change according to time of year, and since variety is the spice of life, this phenomenon makes for better birding. The birds of summer give way to the birds of winter and vice versa, so a new cast of characters takes over on a regular basis. While some birds, such as chickadees, are not migrants but reside year-round within their geographical ranges, the bulk of North American songbirds—and many other birds as well—nest well to the north of where they spend the winter.

Many warblers that nest in the United States and Canada winter in the tropical forests of Central and South America, which is one reason why these forests need to be preserved. Without a winter home, where would a poor bird go? Probably over the brink of extinction. The dark-eyed, slate-colored junco nests mostly north of the Canadian border. From early spring to late fall, this bird is about as rare in the Lower 48 as an ostrich, except in the higher elevations of the Appalachian Mountains. As autumn moves along, juncos leave the north country and settle down south of the border—Canada's, that is—until spring. North Dakota or Massachusetts winters are by no means warm, but areas such as these are included among the places that juncos apparently define as "south."

The forces that trigger the migrations of birds and propel them on their regular long-distance journeys are among the most intriguing mysteries of the animal world. Solving these mysteries has kept many a researcher up all night—partly because that is when many migratory birds travel.

Advantages of migration are obvious. In January, caterpillars are hard to come by in Connecticut or Wisconsin. Yet a tanager, which feeds largely on caterpillars, needs its three squares. What is it to do? Head south, to the tropics, where butterflies abound—and the only way to become a beauteous butterfly is to spend some time beforehand living as a common caterpillar.

Why, then, would a tanager leave caterpillar heaven once the northern winter is over? Certainly not for the exercise. Migratory flights can be wrenching experiences, and many birds perish during these voyages due to dangers such as storms or simply because they run out of steam. (Birds need to stoke up on food before migrating, so keep feeders especially well stocked from early autumn on.)

The migratory urge, as well as the instinct to reproduce, is triggered by hormonal changes in a bird's body chemistry. In temperate areas, seasonal changes in the length of daylight set a bird's juices flowing. But what about in the tropics, where such changes are, at most, slight? Some scientists believe that the beginning of biological preparation for the breeding season is one of the forces that triggers the migratory restlessness that stimulates birds to leave the tropics and start north, even when nesting areas are still frigid.

Migrating birds time their arrival on nesting grounds so perfectly that when they arrive the weather has begun to warm—unless an unexpected late snowfall throws a wrench into the works. At this point, at least a couple of the advantages of migration are apparent. Spring brings an explosion of insect life. Berries and other plant foods frozen during the winter thaw, and new plants sprout. For adult birds with voracious young to feed, it is like a sale at the supermarket. Moreover, most birds are diurnal, and the lengthening day gives them more time to shop.

Over the years, I have marked the turning of the seasons by the migrating birds that visit my yard. I have learned to anticipate the arrival of particular species. Swarms of common grackles alight in the trees during March and October, each bird, it seems, trying to make more noise than any other. The cacophony of their calls drowns out all other sounds. During the late summer and early spring, I know warblers are on the move. Their tiny forms flit among the thickets beyond the lawn, buzzing, and twittering.

Mid-October brings the migrating sharp-shinned hawks. One after the other, sometimes only a minute or two apart, they wing overhead. For twenty-five years—without fail—a pair of red-shouldered hawks arrives as spring approaches, usually in March but occasionally as early as February. Before nesting in nearby woods, they engage in their spectacular aerial courtship ballet, while their screams echo through the sky. I cannot believe the pair I saw last spring were the same as those that were here twenty-five years ago. Although birds of prey can be remarkably long-lived— some eagles have been known to live more than forty years—few die of old age, and even if they do, the chances that they will still be in condition to breed are not very good. It is most probable that when one pair of red-shouldered hawks passes on, another takes over nesting territory in the vicinity.

The return of the red-shouldered hawks was a drama repeated while I was writing this book during late February 1997. I work in the upstairs territory vacated by my children when they fledged and left the nest. My computer desk stands in front of the rear wall of the room, which is largely glass, so while writing I have an excellent view of my backyard lawn, the small pond that lies beyond it, and the woody swamp behind the pond. From my second-floor perch, I have seen an amazing variety of wildlife vignettes—whitetail bucks chasing does, wild turkeys gobbling, otters catching frogs, and great blue herons engaged in the same pursuit, to name a few. On February 27, while seated at my computer, I heard a familiar screaming call outside. I quickly looked up and glimpsed what, for a fraction of a second, seemed to be a winged shadow on the lawn. I craned my neck and looked up and out the window and saw the feathered hunter, my herald of spring, swooping overhead.

For about a dozen years, in the early fall, a single sandpiper spends a day or two skittering around the muddy edges of my backyard pond. I have never seen a sandpiper there at any other time and the bird is always alone. That is proper, because it is a solitary sandpiper. I cannot imagine that it has been precisely the same bird, but I am not able to tell one solitary sandpiper from another. The same is true of the green heron that, for the past several years, has prowled the margins of my pond for about a week each spring.

Just Passing Through

In 1808, America's top ornithologist of the time, Alexander Wilson, arrived in New Haven, Connecticut, with a mission. He was there to peddle his new publication, *American Ornithology*, which became a classic. He found New England distasteful and later noted that his travel there "has rather lowered the Yankeys in my esteem." Perhaps his bad attitude was fostered by the fact that New Englanders are legendary skinflints and he was able to sell only twenty-two copies of his work. At any rate, there were rewards to his trip. He saw tons of interesting birds—and, to his delight, discovered one previously unknown to science.

During October, on the road between New Haven and Middletown, in the central part of the state, Wilson spied a little bird in a thicket. Its back was yellow-olive, while its underparts were pure yellow and its breast greenish yellow. The bird had never been described before. Despite his dislike for "Yankeys," Wilson named it the Connecticut warbler.

You might expect that, given its name, the Connecticut warbler lives in the Nutmeg State. The truth is that it doesn't, except for a short time in the autumn. The Connecticut warbler nests from the Great Lakes across a swath of boreal forest, the vast expanse of coniferous wilderness extending to the northwest across Canada. The only time it has anything to do with Connecticut is during its autumn migration to the tropics.

The story of the Connecticut warbler proves that sometimes you cannot judge a bird by its name. It also illustrates another way in which bird migrations benefit birders. Seasonal migrations give them a chance to see birds that do not nest or winter in their areas but are just passing through.

Unexpected Visitors

Irregular mass movements of several types of songbirds from the boreal forest of Canada into the United States during the winter—which scientists call "irruptions"—also provide backyard bird-watchers with opportunities to view species they normally do not encounter. The birds involved eat fruit and seeds, so feeders will attract them. Many birders pray for irruptions because they give them a chance to see significant numbers of birds that normally do not visit their areas. Among the northern birds that irrupt are some really nifty ones. They include Bohemian waxwings, pine and evening grosbeaks, common and hoary redpolls, red- and white-winged crossbills, and the pine siskin.

It is no mystery why irruptions occur. They happen when the cupboard is bare. The winter food supply can run out for several reasons. Cold or wet spring weather can wreak havoc on the production of the seeds and berries of conifers and other northern trees. Also, even though trees manufacture a bumper crop of seeds and berries one year, they may be less bountiful the next. During the good year, more birds survive, so there are more mouths to feed the following winter.

If a food shortage is localized, there's no problem for the birds in that area. The boreal forest is vast, so they merely move someplace else within the north woods. Major irruptions are triggered when food dwindles across a large area of forest, forcing huge numbers of birds south. Because birds have different dining preferences, irruptions are selective. If birch seeds are short, pine siskins move out. If conifer seeds and berries are hard to find, watch out for invading pine grosbeaks. From year to year, it is a guessing game.

Illegal Immigrants

Many people who feed birds view starlings and, to a lesser degree, house sparrows as pests. There's no question that when a yowling horde of starlings descends upon a feeder, they drive other birds away and act outright greedy. House sparrows, though small, are also belligerent, like that tough little kid with a chip on his shoulder you knew in grade school. Both harass other birds, grabbing their food and driving them from their nesting sites. That is sufficient to engender some animosity on the part of birders, but there is another reason house sparrows and starlings are considered pariahs. Prejudice. Neither is native to North America, and even though they have admirable as well as villainous traits, the prevailing view among birders is that they "just don't belong here."

Blame William Shakespeare for the starling's arrival on these shores. In *Henry IV*, hoping to drive the king crazy until he releases Mortimer from imprisonment, Hotspur says:

> *Nay, I'll have a starling shall be taught to speak*
> *Nothing but "Mortimer," and give it him,*
> *To keep his anger still in motion.*

In 1880, a New York businessman, Eugene Schieffelin, decided to establish in America all birds mentioned in the Bard's writings and released a few dozen starlings in New York City's Central Park. The alien invasion was on—by the 1940s, starlings had reached the West Coast.

House sparrows were imported during the 1860s to combat inchworm infestations in several eastern cities. Like starlings, they prospered in their adopted land. This species, by the way, is not a true sparrow but is a member of a group of birds called "weaver finches."

Introducing exotic species is generally not recommended. However, starlings and house sparrows are here to stay, so we might as well make the best of it. They do have a good side. Both destroy many insects injurious to agriculture and home landscaping. In those city neighborhoods where other birds are scarce, having starlings and house sparrows at the feeder is better than no birds at all. The twittering of a gang of house sparrows is rather pleasant, at least to my ear, and they are sprightly little birds. The white speckles of the starling's winter plumage give it a star-spangled appearance and are responsible for its name. Starlings also can be quite musical. Besides their own ringing wolf whistles, they can mimic the songs of about sixty other birds—and can even meow like a cat and bark like a dog. Whatever. They are now, in effect, naturalized citizens.

Understanding Birds

Even if you are only a casual birder, it is worth learning some basics of avian biology. Understanding what makes birds tick will help you enjoy them more.

3

WHY BIRDS BEHAVE
THE WAY THEY DO

Learn Behavior, Have More Fun

Understanding the behavior of birds—why they do what they do—adds a fulfilling new dimension to bird-watching. If you know even a little about bird behavior, you will be able to recognize and interpret fascinating natural dramas playing out in your own backyard—such as male grackles posturing when they try to intimidate one another, or a male cardinal feeding a female as a token of courtship. Best of all, it is a performance that never ends, although the characters change.

By observing bird behavior you will see intricate natural relationships firsthand. You will come to understand how behavioral adaptations, which have evolved over millennia, help birds—and other animals—survive in the demanding world of nature.

Bird Brains

The term *birdbrain* is unfair. Birds are not ditsy, nor are they simpleminded. Relative to their size, in fact, they have larger brains than any other vertebrates, except for mammals. This is not to say that a bird's brain is designed to operate like that of a mammal. The most highly developed portion of a mammalian brain is its large cortex, the "gray matter" crammed with nerve cells, which is responsible for intelligence and the ability to learn. A bird's cortex is a small, simple structure, poorly supplied with nerve cells. However, nerve cells abound in the massive structure that lies beneath the cortex, the corpus striatum, which controls instinctive behavior.

Since so much of a bird's brain is devoted to instinctive behavior, a bird is ruled by instincts that have been programmed into it over countless generations and are as much products of its evolution as are its shape and physiological processes. A bird can no more change its basic instinctive patterns of behavior than it can alter the color of its plumage. Remember, when you watch a bird going about the daily routine of its life, most of what it does is motivated by instinct, not by reason or emotion. Feeding, courtship, building nexts, and rearing young are all instinctive behaviors.

External cues generally trigger instinctive behavior. The cue may be given by another bird in a form of social interaction. The yawning maws of nestlings, for example, prompt their parents to feed them. Many birds react to a rival's invasion of their nesting or mating territory by standing tall or puffing out their feathers, rather like a boxer trying to stare down an opponent. Male grackles confronting each other rear back their heads and stretch their necks with their bills angled toward the sky so they appear taller and more domineering than is actually the case. Many other instinctive responses result from environmental changes. As noted earlier, drop in air pressure, heralding the approach of a storm, triggers energetic feeding. If you see a large number of birds gathered at your feeding station and eating as if there were no tomorrow, a snowstorm or rainstorm is probably in the offing.

Some instinctive behavior occurs only between members of the same species—a grackle will not strut to bluff a blue jay, only another grackle. However, birds also react to stimuli from species other than their own: a flock of sparrows will veer together almost instantaneously if one of them spots the shape of an approaching hawk. When blue jays grow jumpy and sense a potential danger, they split the air with their loud alarm calls. Nearby jays are alerted and take up the cry. The jays' piercing warnings also make birds of other species jumpy and put them on the lookout for danger. Because blue jays are so common and so vociferous, they can tip off bird-watchers to the presence of an interloper worth observing. When I hear jays sounding the alarm, I take a quick meander around the yard, scanning the skies and nearby trees. Often, I am rewarded by the sight of a bird of prey whose presence has frightened the jays.

The dependence of birds upon instinct does not mean that they are incapable of learning. The natural nest sites of purple martins, for example, are cavities in trees. In the western United States, they continue to depend on trees for

nesting, at least to a large degree. In the East, however, purple martins nest almost exclusively in man-made bird-houses. Why the switch, given that they could still make use of natural cavities? Scientists believe that, long ago, woodland tribes of Native Americans began fashioning nest

Bird-Listening

If you want to be a complete birder, you should be a bird-listener as well as a bird-watcher. Birds can be identified by their songs and calls as well as by their shape, size, and plumage. Learning to distinguish the vocalizations made by different birds isn't always easy, especially if you have tin ear. However, it adds to the enjoyment of birding and can help you determine what birds are in your neighborhood even if you cannot see them.

Although some birds do not sing in the technical sense, virtually all have calls as peculiar to their species as their songs. Although the line between the definition of a song and a call can be blurred, there are some basic differences between the two.

- Generally, a song is a complicated series of rhythmic notes, often delivered in a series.
- Calls are usually individual notes, sometimes uttered singularly, sometimes in a series.
- Songs are mostly restricted to males.
- Calls are voiced by females as well.
- Calls have several functions, including serving as a warning that a predator is near or signaling that food is present.

Some bird voices, such as the "fee-bee" of the eastern phoebe, are quite distinctive and thus easy to identify. Would that all birds were so cooperative. The vocalizations of some species are so similar to those of others that you really must be an expert to differentiate them.

The best way to become proficent is to identify birds first by sight, then by listening to them until you have their voices down pat. There are some excellent audio aids on the market, such as tape cassettes of sounds made by birds, which are valuable learning tools.

boxes for martins out of gourds, possibly in hopes that the birds would return the favor by devouring noxious insects. The martins found artificial nest sites to their liking, and over centuries, their nesting behavior changed.

Birds learn some forms of behavior by imitation. Young birds find the foods they need by watching where adults go to feed. Some young birds develop their songs to their full potential by starting with a rudimentary tune and picking up finer points by listening to the music of adults. Mockingbirds, have the ability to learn the songs of other species in their vicinity and mimic them.

Single Male Robin Seeking Mate

Particularly during the nesting season, male birds go out of the way to advertise their presence. Usually, a male has two objectives: to attract a mate and to warn rivals to keep away. These goals are achieved in several ways. As winter wanes and time to reproduce approaches, the plumage of the male goldfinch gradually begins to brighten from yellowish brown and grayish black, until it is clad in brilliant patterns of yellow and black, as unmistakable to a novice birder as to a female goldfinch. As young male humans frequently do, many male ground birds, such as prairie chickens, strive to arouse feminine interest through elaborate, highly ritualized dances. The form of avian communication most likely to be encountered, however, is song.

Take a male robin, for instance. He can't place an ad in the personals, but he achieves the same effect with his repetitive song. It will draw a receptive female to him, and once she is close, his orange breast will enable her to ascertain that she has indeed found Mr. Right—right species, that is. A male's singing also tells the other males that he is trying to attract the opposite sex and that they had better not interfere.

Stay Out of My Space

As breeding season approaches, many, if not most, male birds seek out a territory to claim as their own. Rather than make the rounds to seek out females, they opt to lure females to their turf. Some birds maintain some form of territory beyond breeding and nesting seasons, but may not defend it as vigorously as when they feel the urge to procreate.

For most backyard birds, song is the first line of territorial defense. Often, the greater a bird's sense of ownership is, the louder his territorial song. The northern cardinal, for instance, is highly territorial, and correspondingly, its song is a loud, clear whistle—which is repeated again and again for emphasis.

Since so much of birdsong is linked to reproduction, spring is when species that nest in North America are most vocal. The eruption of avian music is triggered by the same flowing of hormonal juices that readies the bird's body for sexual activity, prompted largely by lengthening hours of daylight. Not surprisingly, once birds shake out the cobwebs and become active after first light in the spring, myriad species break into what is known as the "dawn chorus." To hear the dawn chorus, you literally have to get up with the birds, but it is worth the effort.

If there is a territorial woodpecker in your neighborhood, you may be awakened in time to catch the dawn songfest whether or not you choose to be. Woodpecker vocalizations are relatively rudimentary, but these birds have another, very effective, way of making themselves heard. They are rappers—not of the gangsta variety, but even so, they can get on your nerves. When a woodpecker is working away at a tree in search of insects, the rhythm of its taps varies, and unless there is a hollow under the bark, the sound is not earsplitting. In the spring, however, woodpeckers really put down the hammer. They seek out a resonant spot, such as a hollow tree, and let loose with rapid bursts of drumming that resemble discharges from an AK-47. If the woodpecker is making its statement on a tree, no problem. Often, however, woodpeckers find houses and gadgets attached to them much to their liking. If a woodpecker decides to use your house as a drumming board, you have a problem.

By way of example, during early spring some years ago, at about dawn, my wife and I awoke to what sounded like a house invasion. The din reverberated through the walls, inside and out, in staccato bursts of sound. A flicker, which is a species of woodpecker, had decided to notify the neighborhood that it had taken up residence by drumming on the tubular rod that supported the television antenna atop our roof.

"Get out [actually, the words I used are not fit for a book on birding], you bird," I shouted. Naturally, I was ignored. The flicker kept pounding for about a half hour, then it departed.

Next morning it was back again. The time had come for drastic measures. I loaded up my favorite side-by-side—for people not familiar with firearms jargon, a side-by-side is a shotgun with two barrels, one next to the other. The devil told me to kill that flicker, but I paid no heed to the dark side and fired into the air. The blast frightened the flicker away—for that morning. Come dawn of the next day, it was back. We had no alternative but to put up with the flicker until it finished making its territorial statement several days later.

An ornithologist I know who is on the staff of the Connecticut Audubon Society tells a story of just how exasperated homeowners can become when woodpeckers sound off on their homes and cannot be discouraged from doing so. One day he answered a telephone call from a housewife who was frantic over such a situation. My friend explained that the woodpecker would eventually go elsewhere and that there was little she could do to hasten its departure. The caller would have none of it. Angrily, she demanded of my Audubon friend, "Well, then, come over here and get your blasted woodpecker."

Territoriality generally dissipates once the young have left the nest. As fall approaches, members of a species that kept their distance from one another may form small flocks. Young birds of the season—a half year away from their first attempt at reproduction—generally lack territorial behavior. During the fall, I have seen as many as six immature cardinals, males and females, gather almost shoulder to shoulder at the same tray feeder in perfect harmony. Their relations come the next spring would not be so peaceable. The males, assuming they survived the winter, would stake out territories and wage song warfare against one another. Trespassers who violated vocal warnings would be chased beyond territorial boundaries.

Territorial singing is designed to avoid conflict. When it fails to do so, birds often resort to aggressive behavior. Those species without the ability to sing are likely to be pugnacious from the get-go. When it comes to bellicose territorial defense, for instance, the hummingbird is a winner. Hummingbirds contesting the rights to airspace will dive-bomb and buzz one another endlessly. Their contentiousness, moreover, extends to birds beyond their own species.

Late one summer, long after the nesting season, I watched a ruby-throated hummingbird go after a blue jay like a Messerschmidt harrying a B-17. The jay's evasive maneuvers were ineffective and it was able to lose its tormenter only by turning tail and heading for the shelter of the trees.

Any Time, Any Place

An experienced birder learns to keep an eye open for fascinating vignettes of bird behavior. And since birds are virtually all around us, you never know when you will see them engaged in some interesting behavior. I have stood on the sidewalks of Manhattan and watched Canada geese and nighthawks migrate overhead. All I had to do to see them was simply look up into the sky. I was rewarded by seeing a touch of the wild in the heart of New York City.

4

BACKYARD BIRDING BASICS

Being a Better Birder

Unless you possess the authority of a Roger Tory Peterson—the late birding legend lived not many miles from me—you can always learn to be a better birder. Since I write about birds, you may assume that I am something of an expert on identifying species and knowing where and how to find them. Perhaps. However, over the years I have burned up the telephone wires asking colleagues at the Connecticut Audubon Society and the Bronx Zoo to help me fix the identity of a bird that I have never seen before and can't quite match with anything in a field book. The fact of the matter is that most people, including "experts," regularly need to draw upon the experience of others to answer birding questions. Never be afraid to ask questions, because most birders are glad to share their knowledge. Try joining a local Audubon society, a bird club, or a nature

center. Bird speciality shops and municipal park depart-
ments often hold programs and field trips for birders that
can be a wealth of information for beginners.

As with other pursuits, the more you understand about
the basics of birding the fewer questions you will have
down the line. If you already consider yourself a proficient
birder, it doesn't hurt to refresh your memory or to pick up
the nitty-gritty details that you should have learned as a
beginner. If, early on in my birding career, I had taken the
admittedly considerable amount of time needed to understand the fine points of optics, I would not have wasted
wads of greenbacks on binoculars that were wrong for
me—and, in some cases, for any birder.

Tools of the Trade

You already own the basic tools of birding—your eyes and
ears. Additional birding aids must be purchased to fully appreciate your subject. There are two that are essential, a
field book—preferably a few field books—and binoculars.

Peterson's *A Field Guide to the Birds* is the granddaddy of
field books. This classic is still among the best. However, it
is not alone. As the popularity of birding has increased, so
has the number of field books. Some of the newer books,
such as *Stokes Field Guide to the Birds* by Donald and Lillian
Stokes, are exceptionally easy to use.

Because no single book has all the information that I
feel is sufficient, I use three field books—the eastern versions of Peterson and Stokes, and *A Guide to Field Identifica-
tion: Birds of North America* by Chandler S. Robbins, Bertel
Brunn, and Herbert S. Zim. Each supplements the others.

Birds in the Stokes guide are depicted in photographs. Those in the other two books are shown in illustrations. Often, you will find that both illustrations and photos are needed to help you identify a particularly troubling bird, especially when it closely resembles another species.

There are also many guides to birds of particular regions of the country and even individual states, which narrows down your research when trying to identify a bird seen in your backyard. Field books for youngsters are on the market as well, and in addition, commercial bird-identification videos are available that, if well produced, can be helpful.

Before buying a field guide, it's a good idea to survey those in the stacks of a library. When you have examined the possibilities, you may try a bookstore, but the chances are that you will find the widest selection—especially among localized guides—at a bird specialty shop.

I have more than one copy of my field guides and keep them within easy reach, next to binoculars, in both my office and my living room, ready to use if I spot a bird on a feeder or elsewhere in the yard that merits closer observation. I also carry a field guide in my truck, in case I encounter an unusual bird while on the road. With ample references at my fingertips, I'm always prepared for an unexpected sighting.

I have found that the old saying about getting what you pay for certainly applies to binoculars. Many novice birders waste money on poor-quality binoculars that give blurry images, are difficult to operate, and can even cause eyestrain. Cheap binoculars are just that—cheap. As a field tool, they are relatively worthless. Quality binoculars, on the other hand, have a comfortable fit for both hand and eye and present images that are bright and sharp. Be pre-

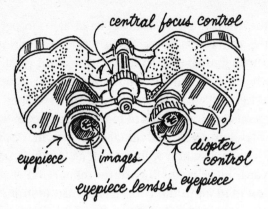

central focus control

eyepiece   images   diopter control

eyepiece lenses   eyepiece

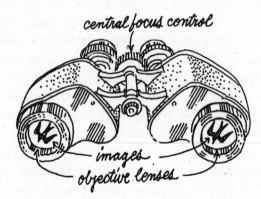

central focus control

images
objective lenses

pared to spend $100 or more—binoculars that are truly excellent cost several hundred dollars—on new binoculars. Making precision lenses and assuring the quality of the various widgets that go into binoculars is an expensive proposition, as opposed to turning out inferior instruments. You may find a good deal on used binoculars at a bird specialty shop. Some of these shops take dandy binoculars as trade-ins from people who are upgrading to the very top of the line. If you opt for this route, make sure the guy behind the counter is reliable and knowledgeable.

Take some time to learn binocular basics and figure out the type that is best for you. You'll save yourself grief later on while investing your money wisely. First off, determine how you intend to use your binoculars. In the backyard only? Or will you take them on birding field trips? Do you prefer to watch birds from a lawn chair? Or will you move around? It all matters. Keep in mind that larger binoculars seem to grow in weight when you are hiking.

Binocular tech talk can be scary for someone who has never encountered it before. The term "eye relief," for instance, has nothing to do with relieving the eyes but is critical to seeing a full field of view. In the simplest terms, eye relief is the distance behind the eyepiece lens where you see the full circle of light that passes through it and contains the image you are viewing. Eye relief is measured in millimeters, and should be at least nine millimeters for people who do not wear eyeglasses and fifteen millimeters for those of us who need assistance. When eye relief is poor, the circular field you are viewing will be obscured around its margins. If you wear eyeglasses, purchase binoculars with foldable rubber cups around each eyepiece. The cups are designed to keep the eyes of someone who does not wear glasses at the proper distance from the lens for correct eye relief. By folding down the cups, you can bring the surfaces of your glasses closer to the eyepiece lens, compensating for the space between your glasses and the pupils of your eyes. This way, you get appropriate eye relief.

Now for the nuts and bolts of binoculars. A binoculars' "power" is the number of times an image is magnified. An eight-power binocular, for example, magnifies an image by a factor of eight, so it appears eight times closer. The number, shown on the body of the binocular, is followed by an × and then another number: for example, 8×42. (The number following the × is the diameter of the objective lenses in millimeters.) Generally, the larger the diameter, the more light a binocular will gather and the heavier it will be, although there are exceptions. Since birders usually ply their trade in daylight, binoculars in the range of 7×35 or 8×40 are often those of choice because they combine plenty of magnification and light with practical size. They supply enough power for the field and more than enough in the backyard. Binoculars with a power of more than ten are relatively large and heavy and are difficult to hold steady enough for birding purposes. Resolution of an image, by the way, decreases with the size of the objective lenses, so compact binoculars are not as sharp as full-size instruments.

Here are a few other points to consider:

- Stick with center-focus binoculars. They are much more convenient than those that require each eye-piece to be focused individually.
- Fixed-focus binoculars are not sharp enough within normal birding ranges.
- A binocular should have a diopter control to adjust for the difference between your strong eye and your weak eye.
- Insist on fully coated lenses, which reduce reflected light loss and thus contribute to a sharp image.

When testing a pair of binoculars in a store, never look out a window. The window glass may distort the image and the bright light could make a low-quality binocular seem more efficient than it will be in a birding situation. Instead, focus on a particular spot within the store where the light is dim but there is plenty of detail. If the image is sharp, open up your wallet.

Getting Started in the Backyard

Once you decide to make your yard hospitable for birds, you should know what birds are likely to be in your area—and when. You will not encounter a Cassin's finch in New York—unless it is badly off course—but you are likely to see one at a feeder in California. If you live in Pennsylvania, cardinals will probably visit your feeding stations year-round, but don't expect chipping sparrows in the winter. Begin looking for them during the spring.

Once you have a feel for the birds that are your neighbors, you may want to concentrate on attracting certain species over others. A feeding station—the feeder and the food it contains—can be tailored to the tastes of particular species. You'll find more on this in subsequent chapters, but here are a few examples:

Tube feeders with perches but without trays are accessible ble to small birds but not to larger species that tend to be more aggressive and push the little guys away from other types of feeders. A tube feeder that lacks perches is even more restrictive and will be used mostly by birds that can cling, such as woodpeckers, finches, and chickadees. Niger seed is especially attractive to finches, but blue jays will largely ignore it. Similarly, some birdhouses have species-specific designs, although they do not always work.

american goldfinch

House sparrows, for instance, often appropriate bluebird houses. Remember that many birds do not use feeding stations or birdhouses. A tube full of sunflower seeds means nothing to an ovenbird because it eats insects, spiders, and other small invertebrates it finds among fallen leaves. Nevertheless, you can still lure ovenbirds and nonfeeder species to your yard by providing plantings that offer food or cover, a subject covered in detail later in this book.

Good Manners

People who feed and watch birds obviously like them. Sometimes, however, birders inadvertently harm the ob-

Quick Tips on Getting Started

- You can start feeding birds at any time of year. The season doesn't matter. As far as birds are concerned, feeding stations are most helpful in winter and early spring, when natural food can be scarce.
- Decide ahead of time where to place your feeder. From what vantage point will you want to view it? A kitchen window? From a patio? Through a sliding glass door?
- Place the feeder where it's easily accessible, not only to the birds but to you. It's not much fun to trudge all the way across your yard through a foot of snow to fill a feeder.

jects of their affection, in the yard as well as in the field. Birders should always remember that the welfare of the birds comes first.

There are scads of stories about how hordes of overeager birders have converged upon an area where a rare bird has been seen, trampled the habitat, and so rattled the poor creature that it left for parts unknown, which might prove less conducive to its survival. Whether in the field or the backyard, never chase birds or repeatedly flush them. Try not to destroy their habitat. Keep your distance from nesting birds. If parents or nestlings act alarmed, beat it.

Once you set out a feeder and fill it, you have assumed an obligation to keep it stocked and clean. There is now some disagreement among experts about the truth of the old axiom that says birds that have become dependent on a feeder during the winter will starve if their supply of seed is suddenly cut off. Still, if you want to call a halt to feeding, it is probably best to wean birds away from your feeder.

How to Tell One Bird From Another

Obviously, if you go through the trouble of attracting birds, you would like to know the identity of the species that visit. Start to acquaint yourself with certain species by learning their distinctive field markings. The most obvious field markings are the color and pattern of a bird's plumage. With some birds, it's easy. If, at first glance, you can't recognize the orange-red breast of an adult American robin, you probably should hang up your binoculars and take up another hobby—Rollerblading, maybe, or bridge. Don't get down on yourself, however, if it takes some effort to figure out the difference between a male and female robin. It's slight. The male has a blackish head, while the female's head, field books will tell you, is lighter, in the range of dark gray. The female's orange-red breast is also not as bright as the male's, but it's only a tad less so. As a rule, male and female robins do not pose side by side so you can compare them, so it can be tough to judge the difference. The juvenile robin can be tricky also. Its breast lacks the full flush of color displayed on the adults and, moreover, it's spotted, which can make a novice birder mistake it for its relatives, the wood thrush and hermit thrush. The plumage of many juvenile birds, notably males, does not resemble its adult form. Young male cardinals, for instance, are brownish like females. The immature rose-breasted grosbeak male lacks the bright red bib of the adult male.

Instead, it is brownish above, like the female, with only a touch of rose on its chest. With sexual maturity, males develop their full adult colors.

If you see a bird with a grayish brown back and a breast colored like a brick, you can determine that it is an adult robin, whatever the sex. Not all birds are so cooperative. The plumage of many species differs radically between the sexes, so you have to get to know both. The male house finch has a red head, throat, and upper breast, its most distinctive field marks. There are touches of red on its back

female house finch 5 to 6 inches

smaller bill

strong streaks

deeper tail notch

white stripe behind eye

dark jaw stripe and cheek

female purple finch 5½ to 6 inches

not as heavily streaked as house finch

as well. Its lower breast and sides are striped with brown. The female has bland, grayish brown plumage, with dark streaks on her sides and underparts.

Quick Tips on Bird Identification

- The body size, and configuration of markings can help you differentiate between look-alike birds. Both the brown thrasher and the wood thrush have brown backs and white breasts with dark markings. The thrasher is three inches longer than the seven-inch thrush, and the bill of the thrasher is strongly curved, which is not so with the thrush.
- Behavior can also be a distinguishing trait. Both the Hammond's flycatcher and the dusky flycatcher share a portion of their respective ranges. While they appear very similar, the Hammond's flycatcher regularly flicks its wings and tail while perched. The dusky seldom flicks its wings, and its tail flicks less regularly than the Hammond's.

Okay, maybe it doesn't seem difficult to tell the difference between male and female house finches, but the story does not end there. House finches closely resemble purple finches, and, in both western and eastern North America, the ranges of the two species overlap, especially in winter. (The house finch was originally only a western bird but has spread throughout the East since it was introduced during the 1940s.)

The purple finch is not really purple. The male's head, throat, breast, sides, and a goodly portion of its back are red,

brown thrasher
10 to 11 inches

yellow
eye

wood thrush
7 inches

spots on breast
blend into
streaks

dark spot on
white
breast

often described as wine-colored, but of a different tinge than the house finch. Still, particularly in winter, when the plumage of both finches fades, the distinction between the two hues of red is not as easy to distinguish as field books suggest. A clue: the male purple finch does not have the strong streaking of the house finch. The females of the two species are more difficult to separate. Female purple finches, like their house finch counterparts, are grayish brown and heavily streaked. One small but significant difference is the white line extending backward from over the eye of the purple finch. The tail of both male and female purple finches is more strongly notched than that of the house finch, but the difference may be difficult to discern unless both species are in view. In my neighborhood, house finches seem to have displaced their purple cousins over the past several years. People regularly tell me they have nesting purple finches that, when checked, turn out to be house finches.

There is no getting around the fact that learning to identify a substantial number of birds is time consuming. Armed with a good field book, quality binoculars, and patience, you can do it. Don't let the difficulties discourage you. In the past, I often went bananas when a bird puzzled me. Bad idea. Birding should never become work; it should always be fun. Even if you are not sure of a bird's identity, you can still enjoy its colors, song, and antics.

5

BEWILDERED BY BIRDSEED?

Junk Food

Being something of a skeptic, I wanted to test the accuracy of a report published in 1980 by the United States Fish and Wildlife Service called *Relative Attractiveness of Different Foods at Wild Bird Feeders.* The report was written by Dr. Aelred Geis, who now is director of research for Wild Bird Centers of America. The study by Geis indicated that many of the seeds commonly sold as bird food, such as corn, milo, and wheat, are next to useless for attracting a wide variety of desirable birds, especially if used in hanging tube and house feeders. These seeds, often used in mixes, are cheap compared to others, such as sunflower, which accounts for their popularity. The problem is, according to Geis, that few songbirds—except for the ubiquitous house sparrows—have a liking for these junk foods, so in the long run, seed is wasted or goes bad, causing sanitation problems. More on that in a moment.

After receiving a wooden tube feeder as a Christmas gift, I decided to experiment. The feeder was described as having been designed for finches and other small birds. Openings in the feeder were not large enough for sunflower seeds, but they were perfect for small grains such as niger. Instructions said to fill the feeder with an appropriate finch mix. I went to the hardware store and bought a small bag of mixed seeds, described on the package as excellent for finches. I hung the feeder near some others that were filled with sunflower seeds. Then I let the sunflower seeds run down. Darned if nary a finch set foot on a perch of my new feeder. They turned up their beaks at its contents. An occasional chickadee sampled a few grains but then departed, seemingly in disgust.

Some of the cheaper mixes do contain sunflower, but only a speckling. These mixes don't work, either. According to Geis, if such mixes are placed in hanging feeders, the birds that use them will grab the few desirable seeds and leave the rest to rot.

Making Sense out of Birdseed

Whatever the merits of the different types and brands, birdseed is marketed with the same intensity as are athletic shoes and soft drinks. The variety on the shelf can be bewildering. White proso millet or black-oil sunflower? Cracked corn or shelled corn? How do you choose? Some basic pointers can help clear up the confusion.

Black-oil sunflower is probably the best all-around bird feed, although in parts of the Southwest finches seem to favor gold proso millet. It is unquestionably the best for standard tube and house feeders, suspended or on poles. Other sunflower seeds, such as striped and hulled, are right up there on the menu as well. Black-oil sunflower was not always the choice for feeding. In fact, at one time it was grown only for processing into oil. The shells were too hard for most birds to crack. Desiring to increase the yield of oil, researchers developed seeds with a thinner shell, thinner even than the shell on striped sunflower seeds. Dozens of different birds can now feed on black-oil seeds, which should be the staple of your bird-feeding efforts, perhaps on a ratio of three to one relative to other types of seed.

Niger is another top choice for small songbirds, particularly goldfinches, which relish it above all else. It is expensive, but birds get only a few grains at a time since the seeds are so tiny they can be dispensed only through feeders with very small openings. (You would not want to put niger on a tray feeder, since a pound can cost a dollar or more.)

White proso millet is a large component of many commercial mixes not fit for a tube or house feeder. However, it has its good points. Although most of the birds that visit tube or house feeders do not relish it, white proso millet is readily consumed by several ground-feeding species, which will also take it from platform feeders. They include juncos, grackles, doves, rufous-sided towhees, red-winged blackbirds, and white-throated sparrows. This millet is a good winter food in much of the country, when migrants such as juncos are abundant in the backyard. Its drawback is that it attracts house sparrows, pugnacious little devils that may drive away birds you would rather see.

When I was a youngster in the Bronx, I would watch old guys sitting on park benches and tossing peanuts to the pigeons. I suspect some of them—the old geezers, not the pigeons—are still there. As feeders of birds, they were ahead of their time. Peanut kernels are catching the fancy of increasing numbers of backyard birders who are willing to pay for them; they are expensive. A neat thing about peanut kernels is that they attract fruit eaters and insect eaters that do not normally dine on other types of birdseed. Some warblers, as well as bluebirds, robins, mockingbirds, and gray catbirds, will opt for peanuts. So will many standard feeder birds, such as jays and several types of sparrows. If you would like to give peanut kernels a shot, you may have to shop around to find them. You probably won't find them at the hardware or feed store. However, ask around at bird specialty shops. Some of them may stock the kernels or can order them for you.

As for corn, most songbirds hate it more than you hated your mother's oatmeal. However, some game birds, such as wild turkeys and ringnecked pheasants, relish it. Be warned, though, that it's sure to bring in crows. Cracked corn, more expensive than the shelled variety, is better, but still no great shakes. As far as the majority of songbirds is concerned, it's still oatmeal—and sunflower seeds are jelly doughnuts.

Quick Tips: Seed You Don't Need

- Canary seed. Save it for the canary.
- Rape. Few birds really take to it.
- Hulled wheat. Ditto.

Mix Your Own

The food preferences of birds vary not only according to species but sometimes by local conditions. Rather than buying a premixed bag of seeds that is marketed from coast to coast, try experimenting with your own mixtures and see if you can develop a blend tailored to the birds in your area. Bulk up the sunflower in the tube feeder with a bit of cheaper millet. The birds that search for the sunflowers will kick the millet onto the ground, where other birds will find it. Try mixing black-oil sunflower with striped sunflower seeds. The black-oil seeds will attract a wide variety of birds, and the striped seeds will be utilized by species that can handle their harder shells. Remember, you can always mix a new cocktail, so experiment.

If you store large amounts of seed you should keep it indoors in a dry, secure place so it will not attract rodents or raccoons. Loose seed should be placed in covered containers so that moths cannot lay their eggs within it. Plastic trash cans with lids that can be tightly secured will do the job. I keep my seed outdoors, in proximity to my feeders. It is stored in large plastic barrels with lids that can be fastened with a clamp-on metal strap.

Specialty Foods

There are several foods that will attract birds with feeding needs that are different or more specialized than those of seed eaters. Hummingbirds will flock to feeders designed for them, filled with imitation nectar. Boil a mixture of one part cane sugar with four parts water. Pour it into the feeder after it cools. If you would prefer not to do the cooking, you can purchase commercial mixtures. In hot weather, empty the feeder every few days if the birds do not drain it, because the mixture can go bad. (My wife, who cares for our hummingbird feeders, says cleaning them once a week is enough.) Wash and rinse the feeder, then refill it. Hummingbird feeders are hot-selling items. Manufacturers engage in continual competition to make a better feeder for the little buzz bombs—and some do work better than others. Many of them are adorned with red plastic flowers, not for aesthetics but because red flowers are very attractive to most species of hummingbirds.

Feeding some birds can be a matter of apples and or-

Quick Tips: Odds and Ends

- Hummingbird feeders attract bees and wasps. Some feeders have devices designed to ward off these insects. Not all of them work. Some people rub Avon Skin-So-Soft, which has become popular as an insect repellent, on their feeders. It won't hurt the hummers.
- The numbers of species you attract depends on the various kinds of food and feeder designs you use.
- If birds don't come to a new feeding station, be patient. They'll find it. Try scattering seeds on the ground as an enticement.

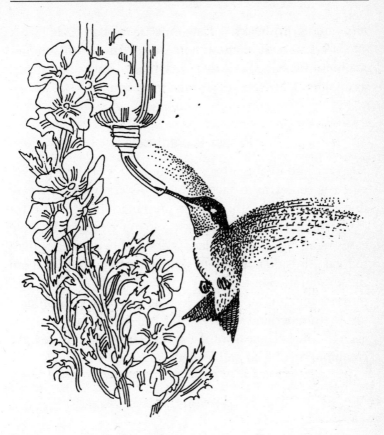

anges. Spike half of an orange or apple on an old log (or whatever), and you have a ready-made feeder. Fruit eaters, such as robins and catbirds, will come to apples. Oranges draw Baltimore orioles and certain woodpeckers. Commercial orange feeders are available.

Many insect eaters—and seed eaters, too—will take advantage of a tray or dish of mealworms, a form of beetle larvae. Among them are bluebirds, wrens, scarlet tanagers, and various grosbeaks. Mealworms are regularly sold by pet shops because they are a staple for many small reptiles. Some fishing bait shops also stock them because "mealies," as anglers call them, are a prime trout bait.

Proper Presentation

The type and quality of seed are only part of the equation when it comes to attracting birds. As chefs who prepare fine cuisine know, the proper presentation of food on a plate counts as much as its taste, so much so that in some cases more space on the plate is devoted to aesthetics than to food. Birds do not take to skimpy portions, but for them the presentation of food is extremely important. The design of the feeder and where it is located can have great impact on the number and variety of birds it will attract. You can even tilt the balance toward a particular species by the right combination of feed and feeder.

6

FEEDER FRENZY

Feeders Galore

If you already are a backyard birder, you don't have to be told that feeder manufacturers produce more models than Santa's elves make toys. There are a mind-boggling number of feeders out there: feeders designed for certain seeds and species; feeders that are suspended; feeders that sit on posts and poles; feeders that go on railings; feeders for the window—ad infinitum. Seeking consumer interest, feeder makers create endless versions and varieties of the standard types of feeders. You can buy feeders with interchangeable bases or divided food containers, both of which accommodate different sorts of birdseed at once. There are feeders surrounded by metal cages that protect the seed from squirrels and shelter the birds that enter it from hawks. You can even find feeders designed to spin on an axis.

Some fanatical backyard birders are often tempted to try feeders equipped with new gadgetry even though the feeders they already have work perfectly well. The search for the perfect feeder is their holy grail. On entering a bird specialty shop, they are in danger of erupting into a feeder frenzy. Beginners can fall into a different sort of money trap by buying feeders with expensive attachments that may be unnecessary.

Whatever its design or purpose, a good feeder should have certain qualities, such as durability and ease of servicing. However, a feeder that is "good" for your neighbor's yard may not be best for you. Assess your own situation before purchasing a feeder.

The Best Feeder

There is no question about the type of feeder that attracts the most birds. Hands down, it's the ground. Many birds, such as juncos and white-throated sparrows, eat on the ground and abhor elevated feeders. Most of the birds that use suspended feeders or those on poles, on the other hand, will also feed on the ground. So, instead of buying a feeder, why not simply sprinkle seed on the ground? Many birders do exactly that, but in combination with feeders. There are some minuses to placing seed on the lawn. Birds feeding on the ground in the open are vulnerable to villainous cats. Seed that is uneaten and remains on the ground for a long time can get messy and go bad. Worse, it may attract rats.

Personally, I take the risks. I dispense seeds on the ground as well as from feeders, and I see more birds because of it. As for the mess, the unattractiveness of seeds on my lawn pales in comparison to the old windows leaning behind the shed that were destined to roof a cold frame, never built, and the five-gallon plastic pails stacked next to them, waiting to be used for something or other. If I lived in a development, which I don't, I would be ridden out of there on a landscaping tie.

However, you may want to assess your own lifestyle and the habits of your neighbors, if you have close neighbors, before feeding birds in a manner that could be considered untidy. Odd as it may seem, there are people who don't give a hoot about birds. A homeowner in a suburb of New York City found that out firsthand. She set up a feeder in her yard, and pigeons were quick to take advantage of it. A neighbor complained to municipal authorities, who came down hard on the bird lover for erecting a structure without the proper permits.

Feeder Facts

Despite the limitless varieties of feeders that are marketed, there really are only a handful of basic feeder types. The tray feeder is a platform that can be put on the ground, a post, a railing, a windowsill, or, in the case of small trays, suspended. Mounted or suspended tray feeders are a good compromise if you want birds that feed on the ground but don't want to scatter seeds there. The flat surfaces of these feeders will tempt birds that shy away from other above-ground seed dispensers. Tray feeders can be roofed or open to the sky. When they have roofs, especially if they have sides as well, they become "house feeders."

Like tray feeders, mounted or suspended bowl feeders attract birds that normally eat on the ground, as well as typical feeder birds. Bowls hold a large amount of seed—

and they need to, because large birds as well as smaller species can use them.

Cylindrical tube feeders, usually made of plastic or wood, but sometimes of wire mesh, are mounted on poles or are suspended. Tube feeders designed primarily for sunflower seeds have ports wide enough to allow birds to extract the relatively large seeds. Tubes for tiny seeds such as niger have much smaller dispensing holes. The perches on tube feeders are usually short enough so that only small songbirds can fit on them, although woodpeckers can cling to them, too. Some tube feeders are mounted atop small trays that prevent seed from spilling on the ground. However, trays also provide perches for large, aggressive birds, such as grackles, that will roust small birds and quickly empty a feeder's contents.

A feeder that mounts on a window is called a window feeder. Window feeders can be crafted of plastic, wood, or a combination of materials. Depending on the model, a window feeder can be affixed to a glass pane with suction cups, mounted on a window ledge, or even set into the window itself. More elaborate varieties often are backed with one-way glass that allows you to see the birds without disturbing them.

Buying Your First Feeder

Almost any general purpose store with room on its shelves seems to sell bird feeders right along with milk and produce, hammers and nails, or lawn mowers and fertilizer. If you are shopping for your first feeder, however, it is probably best to avoid your local hardware or grocery store.

Quick Tips: Things to Consider Before Buying a Feeder

- How durable is it? Like any other device, a feeder should be well made. Beware of flimsy plastic feeders or wooden ones that show shoddy carpentry.
- Will it keep seed dry? Obviously, mesh feeders won't, nor will open tray feeders. Your best bet is a tube feeder or largely enclosed house feeder with holes in the bottom for drainage. Tray feeders with a floor of screening are best.
- Is it easy to clean? Yes, you do have to clean bird feeders. Plastic feeders are easier to wash off than those made of wood.
- How much food will it hold? Obviously, the greater a feeder's seed capacity, the less time you have to spend filling it. Unless a really large feeder is swamped by birds on a regular basis, however, uneaten seed may turn bad. Then you'll have to empty the feeder and clean it.

Head to a birding specialty shop. Chances are that the owner and probably someone on the staff is an ardent birder. Although they are as eager to make a sale as any other merchants, people at bird specialty shops like to encourage new birders, for altruistic as well as economic reasons. In addition, they will have answers that you probably can't get from the guy who sells you salami. Mail-order catalogs from birding products companies are another good place to shop for feeders, and most list a telephone number you can call if you have questions.

Even though a yard with several different types of feeders will draw more birds, try starting off with only one feeder, preferably a small tube that dispenses sunflower seeds. That way, you'll have a feeder that is easy to service and will attract your common perky songbirds. Choose a quality feeder, but one without lots of trimmings. Figure on spending about $25.

Feeders for suet cost only a few dollars. The suet feeder of choice for most backyard birders is a small cage of wire. Hanging suet balls or cakes are also popular.

The more varied the vegetative surroundings of a feeder, the greater potential it has of attracting birds. My feeders are located near brush where birds take cover and trees in which many of them nest. If the location where you first place the feeder doesn't seem to attract many birds, try moving the feeder until you find the best spot. Use your imagination, as one of my neighbors did. He has a feeder suspended from a branch level with an upstairs window and uses a pulley to lower it when it needs filling.

Making Your Own Feeders

If you are handy with tools, you can make your own wooden feeders. State wildlife agencies often will supply plans for feeders—as well as for birdhouses—at a minimum cost. Some of these feeders are rather complicated and definitely require carpentry skills to properly construct.

If you are all thumbs with a hammer and don't know a roofing nail from a brad, don't give up hope. You can still construct some simple feeders. One of them is a log suet feeder, which is just a small log with holes drilled into it to hold suet and a screw-eye on top for suspension.

Certain items of household trash can be recycled into feeders. You can purchase metal fittings, with a perch and a port to dispense seed, that go over the neck of a two-liter plastic soft drink bottle. Just fill the bottle with sunflower seeds, attach the fitting, and hang the bottle upside down.

Doing the Dishes

You don't like eating off a dirty dish. Neither do the birds. However, bird feeders need to be washed far less frequently than table dishes—only about once a month, in fact. Washing them prevents the threat of diseases such as sal-

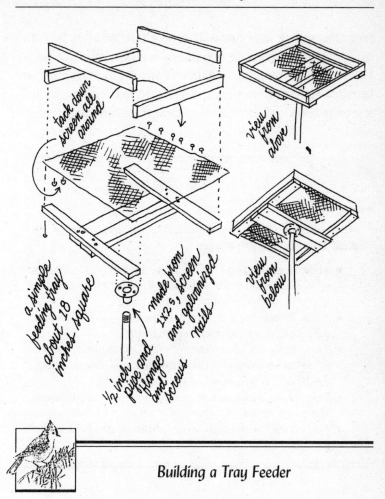

tack down screen all around

view from above

a simple feeding tray about 18 inches square

made from 1x2 s, screen and galvanized nails

½ inch pipe and flange and screws

view from below

Building a Tray Feeder

The tray feeder shown in the illustration is made from a rectangle of screening, a floor flange, and a few pieces of wood. It looks simple, yet the job of stretching the screening is no easy feat. Still, the materials cost much less than the price of a store-bought feeder of similar design.

monella, which can grow in seed that becomes wet and moldy. Clean feeders in hot, soapy water with an ounce or two of chorine bleach to a gallon of water. You can purchase brushes especially designed for scrubbing feeders, including brushes with long handles for use on tube feeders.

The Right Stuff

Here are some feeder-seed combinations and some of the birds they are likely to attract.

- Tube feeder with black-oil sunflower: goldfinches, woodpeckers, titmice, chickadees, nuthatches, pine siskins, house finches, and lots, lots more
- Tube feeder with niger: goldfinches, purple finches, pine siskins, chickadees, house finches
- Tray feeder with millet: doves, blackbirds, white-throated sparrows, white-crowned sparrows, juncos, towhees, tree sparrows, chipping sparrows
- Tray feeder with cracked corn: grackles, white-throated sparrows, doves, jays, juncos
- Bowl feeder with sunflower: cardinals, grosbeaks, blue jays, as well as smaller birds

It's Your Choice

The bottom line on feeders is that you don't have to be swept away by a frenzy of buying, building, and erecting every variety imaginable. Pick the right kind of feeder and match it with appropriate seed to attract the birds you enjoy seeing most. Even one feeder will make your yard more bird friendly. Of course, the more elements birds require to live that you add, the more of them will be seen outside your window.

7

GIVE A POOR BIRD
A HOME

Maternity Wards for Birds

Speaking in the strictest technical terms, a "birdhouse" isn't a house at all. It is a nest box in which certain species of birds—you hope—will build their nests and rear their young during the spring and summer. True, birds will use nest boxes for shelter at other times of year—you can put out roosting boxes, better designed for this purpose—but, basically, a nest box is a maternity ward and nursery all in one.

I have only two nest boxes in my yard, one for bluebirds and another for house wrens. I don't concentrate on boxes because I have plenty of nesting habitat in and around my yard, including dead trees, large conifers, and brushy tangles, so that many birds nest on my property naturally. Nest boxes, however, are especially useful in yards that lack the type of natural surroundings that birds will occupy when they are approaching a blessed event.

Nest boxes will not attract nearly as many birds as feeders. Most backyard birds, in fact, do not use nest boxes, at least not on a regular basis. Orioles, cardinals, and doves are among the species that avoid boxes. Still, more than two dozen species—including some that do not visit feeders—will take advantage of one sort of nest box or another. Bluebirds, in particular, benefit from boxes because their natural nesting sites in tree cavities have become scarce and are often taken over by aggressive house sparrows and starlings. Bluebird numbers were in decline, but these pretty creatures have made a comeback because conservation organizations have encouraged people to put up boxes that give bluebirds a home during the nesting season.

Dream Homes for Birds

When it comes to choosing a dream house, birds are as picky as people. Just as human parents shop around for a home in a good neighborhood, with low taxes, and in an excellent school system, birds are very demanding about where they raise their young. Some nest boxes are used by a number of different species with like requirements; as a rule, however, if you want to attract a particular bird you have to put out a box designed especially for it—and make sure it is in the right location.

Birds set up housekeeping in digs that mimic the nest sites they use in nature, which can vary immensely from species to species. Bluebirds, chickadees, and house wrens, for example, are adapted to nesting within cavities in trees, including holes abandoned by woodpeckers. A box for these species should have the same feeling of shelter and security as an old woodpecker hole. Bluebirds and chickadees do not like roomy bedrooms; they opt for a room that is small and cozy. Since barn swallows and phoebes nest on ledges, they will not use a box. Furnishing a simple open platform, with or without a roof, will entice them to nest.

Building Code for the Birds

Even though the individual requirements of various species differ, there are basic elements of good nest box design and construction—a building code for the birds, if you will. They hold true whether you buy a commercial nest box or build one yourself. A surprising number of different materials go into the construction of commercially built nest boxes, stuff like rubber, plastic, recycled paper, and metal, as well as the old standby, wood. Of them all, wood is probably the best because it is durable, it insulates, and it breathes. The wood for a nest box can be slab, rough-cut, or finished wood. One is as good as the other, except that finished wood may be slippery for birds entering and leaving the house through the opening. A few grooves below the hole, inside and outside, will correct the problem.

The United States Fish and Wildlife Service recommends three-quarter-inch bald cypress and red cedar as the top woods for nest boxes. Pine and exterior-grade plywood are okay as well but should be covered with a coat of water-based exterior latex paint for durability. The inside of a nest box should never be painted or stained because the chemicals in paint and stain may be harmful to its tenants. Boxes with joints glued together and with galvanized or brass

nesting box

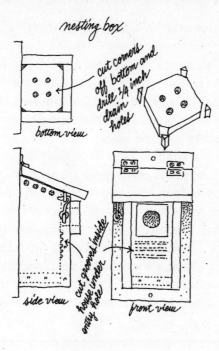

bottom view

cut corners off bottom and drill 1/4 inch drain holes

side view

cut grooves inside house under entry hole

front view

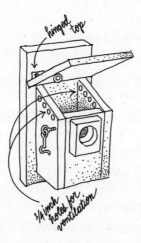

hinged top

1/4 inch holes for ventilation

screws and hardware will last the longest of any made out of wood.

If a nest box is not properly ventilated, its primary function once the hot sun begins to beat down will be to cook birds. Ventilation can be provided through quarter-inch holes in the sides just below the roof or by narrow gaps between the roof and the sides.

A nest box should be built to prevent water from entering. A roof that slants either from its apex or from back to front, and has an overhang, will shed rain. In case water does happen to get into the box, the right floor design can prevent it from pooling. Ideally, the corners of the floor of a nest box should be cut at the corners on an angle, instead of squared, and punctured with a few small holes. Speaking of holes, a nest box should never have a perch below its entrance because it could help predators gain access to its interior.

Quick Tips: Color Preferences

- Purple martins are attracted to white houses.
- Most other hole nesters, such as wrens, like tan, gray, or dull green.
- Bright colors should be avoided because they may attract predators.

Being a Good Landlord

A nest box should be easy to open—not by the birds but by you. One of the services that you occasionally should supply for your avian tenants is to clean out the house. Of course, the box should not be disturbed while nestlings are inside, except in an emergency. Just in case you have to look in before the young have fledged, a box that opens from the top is safest because the nestlings are not in danger of falling out.

The time to clean out the contents of the box is once the nest is empty. Remove the old nesting materials. Check the floor for fleas, mites, and insect larvae. If they are present, hit them with an insecticide that will not harm birds, such as 1 percent rotenone powder or pyrethrin spray, because another family of birds may take up residence once the original lodgers have departed.

Placing the Box

Exact placement of a nest box may depend on the species of bird it is intended to attract. However, there are some givens for boxes in general. Never tilt the box so that its hole faces upward or rain will enter it. Keep the box level—or, better yet, at a slight downward angle. As a rule, the box should not be exposed to the full force of the sun for long periods of time. Boxes can be mounted on posts or trees. Many birds prefer boxes attached to the limbs, rather than trunks, of trees, since they naturally build their nests in the branches.

A tree should hold only one box for a particular species to prevent conflict over territory. Spacing between boxes is very important. For instance, bluebird boxes should be a hundred yards apart and there should be no more than four boxes for any one species per acre.

A Place to Roost

Roosting boxes can provide shelter for birds during rough winter weather. Roost box requirements are not as precise according to species as are those for nest boxes. Use the same sort of wood and other materials to build a roost box as you would a nest box. The interior dimensions of a roosting box should be about ten by ten inches, its height about three feet. The entrance hole can be two to three inches in diameter. To make perches, glue quarter-inch dowels into holes drilled through the sides of the box. Hinge the roof.

Preferred Tenants

Bluebirds are among the most prized residents of nest boxes. They are mainly country residents, but if you live in a heavily populated area near a golf course or a cemetery—cemeteries are prime birding spots—you still may be able to attract them. Bluebirds wanting, house sparrows will almost certainly show up as squatters.

Bluebirds prefer to nest in boxes on a tree stump or a post between four and five feet high. A post is better because it can be guarded against predators (see chapter 9) with a circular baffle or a sheath of metal, if the post is wooden. The best spot to put the post is in or near a field. My neighbor has had tremendous success with bluebird boxes in his hay field, a beautiful sward of green that he tends more meticulously than most suburbanites do their lawns.

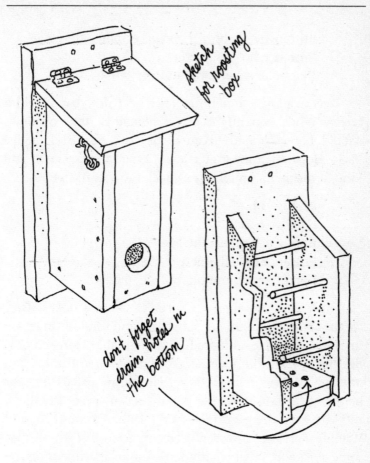

sketch for roosting box

don't forget drain holes in the bottom

The entry hole of a bluebird box should be an inch and a half in diameter, which is too small for starlings to enter. The dimensions of a bluebird box—for eastern, western, and mountain species—are as follows (in inches, except for the height above ground level, which is given in feet).

Width: 5 by 5
Height: 8 to 12

Entrance hole height above bottom: 6 to 10
Entrance hole diameter: 1½
Height above ground, in feet: 4 to 6

Tree swallows sometimes take over deserted bluebird boxes. While you might prefer bluebirds, tree swallows should be welcomed because they are beautiful, active birds. However, they prefer boxes especially designed and located for them, preferably attached to a dead tree.

Width: 5 by 5
Height: 6 to 8
Entrance hole height: 4 to 6
Entrance hole diameter: 1½
Height above ground, in feet: 5 to 15

Chickadees are almost a sure bet for nest boxes. They can be abundant in urban, suburban, and rural settings; are unafraid of people; and are highly adaptable. Hang chickadee boxes from limbs or secure them to tree trunks. You probably should follow the specifications listed here for height of the box above the ground because, like all others, they are from the good folks at the United States Fish and Wildlife Service. However, from experience, I know that some chickadees will readily settle for an apartment on the first floor, rather than higher up. One family nested inside a hollow stump on my lawn no more than two feet above the grass. Titmice and nuthatches have feeding and nesting habits similar to those of chickadees, so don't be surprised if one of these species tries out the nest box.

Width: 4 by 4
Height: 8 to 10
Entrance hole height above bottom: 6 to 8

Entrance hole diameter: 1 high, 2 long
Height above ground, in feet: 4 to 15 (but cleaning out a box 15 feet up is not easy)

House wrens like a box with an entrance that is a slot rather than circular, although they will use a round entrance. Other than that, they are not very particular in choice of a small nest box as their pad for the season.

Width: 4 by 4
Height: 4 to 6
Entrance hole height above bottom: 4 to 6
Entrance hole diameter: 1½ high, 2½ long
Height above ground, in feet: 5 to 10

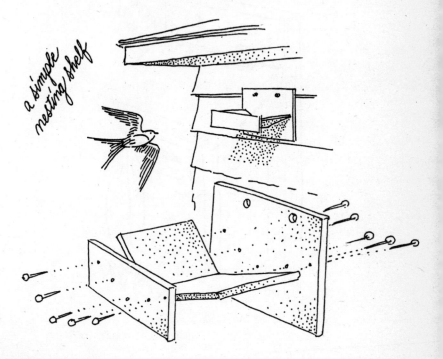

a simple nesting shelf

They Want a Platform

Our house has large, overhanging eaves supported by large wooden beams that run the length of the building. Almost every spring, a pair of barn swallows or phoebes plasters a nest against the beam protruding from the exterior wall. Whichever of the two species arrives first takes the rights to the spot. Usually it is the phoebes.

Phoebes are great birds to have around. They are pleasantly vocal and active as they perch on tree limbs and fence

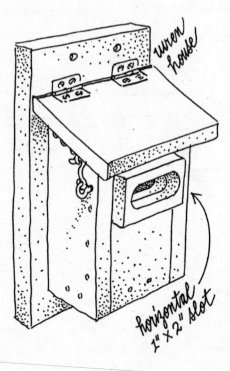

wren house

horizontal 1" X 2" slot

posts and then dart into the air to collar flying insects. Although it is not a good idea to disturb birds on nests, you can get remarkably close to nesting phoebes—even see their young—without rattling them. The grace and beauty of barn swallows as they swoop through the air after insects is legendary. Given their inclination for eating insects, both species are natural pest controllers. Barn swallows and phoebes do not nest in boxes but will use platforms attached to the sides of building. Robins may take advantage of a platform on a building, but more often than not they prefer ones attached to the trunk of a tree.

Coupled with feeders, nest boxes will enhance the value of your yard for birds. You can really complete the package by providing them with additional attractions, such as food and cover plantings and water, which are discussed in the next chapter.

8

NEAT AND NATURAL WAYS TO ATTRACT BIRDS

It's a Jungle Out There

There was a time when setting out a feeder or two, and perhaps a nest box, qualified a person as a hard-core backyard birder. No longer. Increasingly, real birding aficionados are looking upon part or even all of their landholdings as bird sanctuaries. Encouraged by conservation organizations, people are converting their yards into habitat for birds and, for that matter, other kinds of wildlife.

Note, however, that if you create a backyard Eden for wildlife, you may not appreciate some of the critters that decide to populate it, like skunks and snakes. In Montana, state wildlife authorities do not encourage landowners to allow dense brush near their homes. The reason? Cougars tend to find it comfy.

Even if you do not want a real jungle out there, there are lots of neat steps you can take to attract birds the natural way. Some take work, but others can get you out of odious tasks such as mowing the lawn.

Essential Stuff

A backyard that is really for the birds should have the complete package of essentials they need to survive. If you have a feeder, you are already providing them with some food, but you can add plantings that produce seeds and fruits. Providing water for bathing and drinking can be as easy as filling up a plastic trash container lid and placing it on the ground or securing it to a low post. Cover that shelters birds from predators, competitors, and the weather, while giving them a place to rear young, can be created in many ways. Cover includes sites where birds can perch and where males can display and sing. An oak tree on the far bank of my pond caught my eye when I noticed that one particular branch was dying. I considered trimming off the limb but never got around to it. One April day, I watched a female red-shouldered hawk—half of the pair that come to our yard each spring—perch there. A few minutes later, the male arrived and perched next to her. Moments after that, they mated. If I had removed the branch, I probably never would have witnessed an event that, from a birder's standpoint, is memorable.

If you offer birds habitat that suits them, they will enthusiastically accept your invitation—and you'll probably have to increase spending on birdseed because the water and cover will bring more birds to your feeders.

Sounds Like a Plan

Any effort to improve bird habitat in the backyard should be thought out very carefully. I speak from experience. Over the years, certain hasty and ill-planned attempts to enhance the value of my yard as bird habitat have been disastrous. My first encounter with bee balm, which hummingbirds love because it is sweet scented and red, their favorite color, is a prime example. Bee balm grew on several sites in my woods. Wanting hummingbirds close to the house, I transplanted a few shovels full of bee balm into a flower bed near the deck outside our living room.

Bee balm is an invasive perennial. Once the gate is opened to a few bee balm plants, they become a Fifth Column. They produce an invading horde that chokes out the previous occupants of a bed. I knew that bee balm was a take-over kind of plant but underestimated its ability to control its turf. I lost some treasured perennials in the bed to the onslaught of bee balm and had to redig it completely. Many bee balm plants perished in the process, but some I saved, deporting a bunch of them back to their place of origin, the woods. It was easy. Bee balm is so tough that all one has to do is dig up a clump of it in a shovel and plop it somewhere else on the ground—perhaps score the earth on which it is dropped—and it will take root, live long, and prosper.

Unrestricted plantings of bee balm are suited only to wild corners of the yard, where plants can wage their game of competition and you do not have to act as referee. If you want bee balm in a bed, you have to confine it. Naive as I was, I never thought of planting it in large pots and sinking them into the earth.

Before you begin to create a backyard bird sanctuary, take stock of all the habitat elements on your property. Note the plants that are already there, their locations, and whether or not they are advantageous as food and cover for birds. Are shrubs clumped so as to provide good cover or are they spaced too far apart? What types of food plants do you have? Is there an area you can allow to revert to the wild? Does the yard have any rock structure, either natural or artificial? If you need help figuring out what your yard has to offer in terms of bird habitat, there are plenty of places to get advice, such as your state wildlife agency, local birding groups, and possibly your area's Cooperative Extensive Service. A great source of information is the National Wildlife Federation's Backyard Wildlife Program (8925 Leesburg Pike, Vienna, Virginia 22184). Garden and landscaping shops can also be of assistance, but remember that they have a vested interest in your pocketbook.

Next, make a sketch of your entire property—to scale, if you can. Include all natural elements, as well as your house and any other structures, fences, or walls. Once the yard is diagramed, decide on alterations and additions, both long and short term, that you would like to make and add them to the sketch.

You may find that some existing plantings can be rearranged to enhance the yard's habitat potential, but it is likely that you will also have to add others. Check space requirements for plantings. Will the plants you have in mind still have enough room when they mature several years down the road? How long will plants take to reach a size where they are useful to birds? Will cover attract rabbits that will feed on your vegetable plants? If you install one of those little backyard mini-ponds, how do you keep

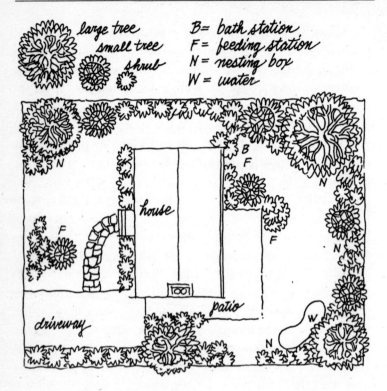

large tree
small tree
shrub

B= bath station
F= feeding station
N= nesting box
W= water

N

B
F

house

N

F

F

N

driveway

patio

W

N

it from becoming mosquito heaven? How much lawn do you need? Be sure that any alterations that make your yard more hospitable for birds will not be undesirable for people. After all, you and your family have to live there, too.

A landscaping plan for birds should contain open areas, including lawn, interspersed with and bordered by woody plants. The juxtaposition of the two creates what wildlife managers call "edge habitats." The diversity of wildlife where two types of habitat meet is greater than that within either of them, because the interface contains a mixture of cover and food derived from both. The edge should be irreg-

ular because that creates more of it than a straight line—
and straight lines can be dull to look at. Try using islands
of shrubs or flowers scattered about the lawn. If you have
a small yard, restrict dense thickets to the corners or a side
of the property. Make use of the plants you already have;
they can be core plants to which new ones are added or
they can be transplanted. If you add plants, make sure they
are natives, which support a much greater variety of wildlife than exotics.

Quick Tips: Before You Plant

- Think seasonally. Evergreens are a key cover during the
  winter, when the branches of deciduous trees are bare.
- Mix plants that fruit in the summer and fall. Include
  plants, such as hawthorne and ornamental crab apple,
  with fruits that remain on the branches all winter.
- Many weeds retain seeds in the winter and well into
  early spring.

Gardening for Birds

Gardening is the only hobby in the country with more ad-
herents than birding. Since combining the two hobbies is a
natural progression, many gardeners are also birders. It is
difficult to find a seed catalog without a section on plants
that attract birds or a birding catalog that doesn't offer
plants.

Without a doubt, gardening for birds doubles the pleasure for a person who is interested in both. It also increases the toil. Backyard birders who are also gardeners fight battles on two fronts. On one hand, they must counter the squirrels that ravage feeders, while on the other, they wage constant combat against the chickweed that smothers vegetable beds. (Actually, some birds love to eat chickweed and may turn the tides in this particular battle.) The extra work is worth it, however, because gardening and backyard birding go together like that proverbial horse and carriage.

The term "gardening," as used here, must be taken in its fullest context. It includes planting and caring for trees and shrubs as well as flowers—the full spectrum of cultivated plantings, if you will. Coniferous trees and shrubs, and other evergreens such as holly, are super selections because their foliage provides year-round shelter and should be a part of any backyard bird habitat. Traditionally, many homeowners consider coniferous shrubs such as yews and junipers to be foundation plantings or hedges, which are regularly manicured, but birds benefit much more from these plants when they grow in patches, uncut.

Large coniferous trees are pretty much unbeatable as shelter for a host of songbirds. In my backyard grows a massive Norway spruce that is a veritable apartment house for birds. On winter nights, it shelters scads of birds that are either year-round residents or migrants from the north. It is alive with birds during the spring. Nesting within its boughs are mourning doves, common grackles, robins, house finches, and, I suspect, other species as well.

A skyscraper of a spruce, of course, may not be practical for many backyard habitat plans. Not every yard has sufficient space to accommodate such a majestic tree. Moreover, the seedlings of trees in general take several years to grow to a stage at which they will attract birds. Our spruce was already quite sizable when we moved in almost thirty years ago, and I estimate that it is about fifty years old. Slow-growing trees, such as oaks, take much longer to reach full height—a couple of hundred years, in some cases.

Disadvantages of large trees aside, if you have the space and the patience, they should be considered when you are planning a backyard habitat. Many trees are as valuable for the foods they produce as they are for the shelter they offer. For instance, almost fifty species of birds feed on something or other from the eastern white pine alone. Brown creepers, evening grosbeaks, and goldfinches are among the birds that eat its seeds. Wild turkeys eat the needles. Yellow-bellied sapsuckers—naturally—suck up the sap.

Plants that bear fruits and berries are an essential part of backyard bird habitat. Chokeberry and Mongolian cherry, which form thickets that create sites for nests, are also prime summer food sources for birds that enjoy fruit. So are raspberries, but if your crop is good, you will probably give in to selfishness, shoo away the birds, and eat the berries yourself. In the fall, if you should see birds eating berries and then flying erratically, pull them over and give them a citation. They may be flying under the influence. Some fruits ferment, and the birds that eat them can get boozed up. A horticulturist I know told me that he regularly sees birds lying on the ground under his mulberry tree that are so stoned they are literally paralyzed.

A flower garden also can be a good source of food for birds. Songbirds such as juncos, finches, and cardinals relish the seeds of many garden flowers. Among these plants are coreopsis, marigolds, zinnias, and black-eyed susans. I always leave some black-eyed susans and marigold plants standing when I batten down my flower gardens for the winter. The best flower to plant for birds is, understandably, the sunflower. With so many dwarf sunflower varieties available, you do not need a large amount of space for this premier seed producer.

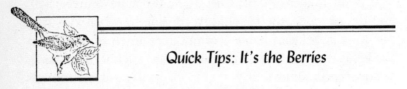

Quick Tips: It's the Berries

Here are some plants that fruit at different times of the year.

- Early summer: red mulberry, service berry, black raspberry
- Fall: viburnums, dogwoods, spicebush

Nongardening for Birds

Cut down on chemical, noise, and air pollution. Save money. Have more time to play golf—or watch birds. Anger fastidious neighbors. You can accomplish all these goals while attracting birds if you let your lawn grow into a wildflower and weed field. All you have to do is sit back and watch the grass grow. No more lawn chemicals. Good-bye noisy, foul-smelling power mower. Let nature take its course.

Well, maybe not entirely. You probably want to retain some lawn, especially close to the house. And even after the lawn reverts, it still needs some care. You probably will have to cut it once a year—I find early spring is best—to keep more aggressive plants from taking over. To maintain species diversity, you may have to remove domineering species on occasion.

Once a patch of lawn remains uncut for even part of the growing season, other plants beneficial to birds will move in. Forget-me-nots, buttercups, and other wildflowers will fleck your backyard meadow. Birds will come flocking, because a lawn growing wild contains many more insects—and cover to protect them while they feed—than a lawn that is regularly mowed.

Letting lawns or portions of them grow wild has found increased favor among nature lovers. But it has its opponents, too. Neat-freak neighbors may complain. Some stuffy municipalities have even passed laws against naturalizing lawns, so check your local ordinances.

Another way to naturalize your lawn, although it takes work, is to replant it as a wildflower field. The quickest way is to till up the lawn—preferably in the fall, then again in early spring—and plant it with a mixture of wildflowers and grasses. You can buy mixes from catalogs, garden shops, and hardware stores. Be sure the mix contains only seeds of plants native to your area. At first, you have to care carefully for the field—watering it, for example, and removing unwanted plants that have sprouted from seeds that entered the soil beforehand. Know, too, that wildflower mixes are by no means surefire. Results even with a good mix will be sparse the first year, but if the field takes, the next year will produce glorious wildflowers.

I tried a variant on a wildflower field when I had to clear a large expanse of trees and brush to install an engineered septic system. I waited for nature to take its course and watched to see what types of plants arose from the bare soil. I also plugged in a few daylilies and bee palm plants.

By late summer, my "weed field" was lush. Asters proliferated. A milkweed stand was spreading. The yellow of goldenrod was evident. Goldenrod, by the way, gets a bad rap. It doesn't cause allergies. Ragweed does. During the winter, the seeds of wild goldenrod are a key food source for several species of sparrows, as well as goldfinches, pine siskins, and juncos.

The vegetation in my field was up to my shoulders. Bees of every description buzzed among the foliage, and butterflies loved it. By late fall, hordes of juncos and wintering sparrows rustled through the dry weed stalks, gorging on seeds. Eventually, however, asters took over and practically eliminated other species. I took out a brush cutter just this past spring and leveled the vegetation. I can't wait to see what comes up next.

Brush Piles Are Beautiful

Many people consider brush piles eyesores, but for birds and other wildlife they make beautiful cover. If you live in an area where venomous snakes are common, you may want to discard the idea of building a brush pile. Even if snakes are not a problem, you need to own a fair share of property to use brush piles as a tactic for attracting birds. Just bear in mind that the piles should be a good distance from your house—perhaps fifty yards as a minimum.

It doesn't take an architect to make a brush pile. Put the heaviest branches—with the addition of a log or two—on the bottom. Toss in a few rocks to help anchor the pile.

Know What You Eat

By the way, if you are watching your backyard birds feed on wild fruits and berries, don't believe the old garbage about how, if you are lost in the woods and hungry, you can safely eat what the animals eat. Cardinals, catbirds, and sparrows enjoy the berries of nightshade. Do as they do and you will end up in the hospital or even in a coffin, because nightshade contains a toxin called solanine, which—to put it mildly—is very bad for your body. Similarly, bluebirds, magpies, and chickadees set a really bad example when they eat the berries of poison ivy.

Stack the brush with the cut ends of branches toward the ground. Throw a few larger branches on top to keep the pile in place. It is a smart idea to scatter some weed plants and dead flower heads into the pile. Their seeds will feed the birds, and some of them may sprout the next spring. A brush pile can be dressed up a bit by planting vines, such as Virginia creeper and bittersweet, around its margins.

To make a brush pile, of course, you need a source of brush. A good time to start your brush pile is after you have cleared land or taken down even one tree. Occasionally, trees have to be felled. In some ways, I would rather take down a live one than a tree that is dead. A bevy of birds—such as screech owls and bluebirds—nest in cavities within dead trees. Woodpeckers and many other species feed on insects in the decaying wood. Many mammals also use dead trees for a variety of purposes. If you appreciate wild-

life, there are only two real reasons for cutting down a dead tree:

1. It may fall on your house.
2. It may fall on your neighbor's house, which is worse because you could land in court.

If you have the space to leave dead trees alone, by all means do it. They are a prime part of woodland habitat.

Belly up to the Bar

Like many humans after a hard day's work, birds gravitate to watering places. They need water not only to drink but to keep their feathers in good condition, to relieve the itch and discomfort caused by mites and lice, and to cool off. You can give birds water in a basin on the ground or in a raised birdbath. Either way, the container should have a slightly rough surface so that the footing is not slippery,

Down and Dirty

Birds like to get down and dirty. They hunker into dry soil to take dust baths that rid them of external parasites. Birds need sandy grit, too, which is why you may see them picking up sand by the roadside. Grit enters a bird's gizzard and helps it to grind up food. Therefore, dust and grit are added attractions for birds. Try filling a tray, a couple of feet square, with sand or a mixture of sand and fine soil and placing it near your bird feeder. Or simply till up a patch of soil about the same size and keep it loose.

and the water should be no more than three inches at its deepest point.

A mini-pond for birds can be made by lining a plastic trash can lid with cement and either placing it on the ground or setting it into the soil. This sort of pool can be especially attractive if it is adorned with rocks and set into a flower garden.

Water containers for birds should be washed out at least twice a week to eliminate mosquito larvae and clean out droppings and other debris. There is at least one product on the market that prevents birds from fouling their drinking water. The bowl containing the water is covered by a lid. Birds drink through a hole in the lid without actually entering the water. The bowl containing the water rests within a larger outside bowl. The airspace between the two bowls insulates the water from extreme temperatures, so when the container is placed in the sun, passive solar heat keeps it from freezing in air temperatures as low as 20 degrees Fahrenheit.

A leak from a broken faucet may drive you crazy, but birds love the sound of dripping water. The gentle splash of water can cause a marked increase in bird visitors. Several different devices, such as recirculating pumps and special garden hose attachments, can be used to move water in a birdbath or pool. You can get the same effect by hanging a leaky bucket or perforated plastic bottle over a bath. A heavy elastic band around the bottle will increase the drip. Many garden shops sell kits for making attractive bird pools complete with a pump that circulates water. Freezing winter temperatures complicate the task of watering birds. You can regularly refill your watering hole with warm water and melt the ice or keep the water from freezing with an electric heating element made for the purpose. Some birdbaths even come equipped with electric heaters.

Your Own Eden

Once you have landscaped your yard for birds, you will have to maintain it now and then, but if you planned properly in the beginning, you won't have to break your back. The rest of the time, you can sit back, smell the flowers, and enjoy the color and songs of birds in your own little Eden.

9

BIRD BUTCHERS AND BACKYARD BANDITS

Good Kitty, Bad Kitty

Americans are bonkers for pets. We own about 54 million dogs and at least that many cats, not to mention the multitudes of feral felines that prowl woods and back alleys. We pamper their palates with "beefy chunks in beef gravy" and "burger . . . with real cheese flavor and protein-rich egg." There are baby-sitters, livery services, and even psychiatrists for pets, and it is likely that many of the patients seen by pet shrinks are desperately confused cats—all because of birds.

Think about it. If kitty kills a mouse in the pantry, kitty is good; if kitty whacks a sparrow under the feeder, kitty is bad—and even worse if the victim is a cardinal or an evening grosbeak. The emotional distinction that a human may make between one creature clad in fur and another in feathers is lost on a feline. From a cat's perspective, both are equally viable choices as prey.

A few pet cats have it all figured out. They ignore birds, at least when their owners are watching, and concentrate their predatory energies on mice that leave presents in the cupboard and moles that uproot the lawn. They wisely bring the trophies of the hunt home and prance around in front of their providers with mangled little carcasses in their jaws. Good kitties, indeed.

However, the average cat is a bird junkie, an addiction it learns early in life. For this sort of cat, the backyard feeder—and birdbath, too—can be a fast-food restaurant. A towhee with its head down and tail pointing skyward as it eats birdseed on the ground triggers the feline equivalent of a Big Mac Attack.

Once a cat is hooked on birds, the odds are that it will become a serial killer. If you figure that there are millions of such cats in the United States, the toll they take must be astronomical—several million birds a day, according to some estimates. A four-year study in Wisconsin several years ago suggested the magnitude of the slaughter. Cats there, researchers said, dispatched 19 million songbirds and 140,000 game birds annually. Those were some really bad cats.

The cat that probably was the baddest of all belonged to a lighthouse keeper on tiny Stephens Island, off New Zealand. One day in 1894, it came home carrying the corpse of a little bird that the keeper had never seen before. Neither, it turned out, had anybody else. As weeks passed, the cat showed up with a dozen more. Then the killing stopped, not because the cat decided to show mercy but because the supply of birds ran out. Scientists eventually determined that the cat's victims were the last individuals belonging to a type of wren, endemic to Stephens Island, which had been previously unknown to them. The lighthouse keeper had witnessed an event of cosmic proportions. His cat had killed off an entire species.

Obviously, someone who likes to watch birds and also has a cat that likes to eat birds has a problem. How can the dilemma be resolved? Not easily. Declawing the cat will help, but it still will be able to bat down birds and then seize them in its jaws, and, besides, removing a cat's claws is cruel. A bell around the cat's neck won't work, either. Birds do not associate a ding-a-ling or jingle with a predator.

There are a few solutions, albeit not simple ones. Don't get a cat in the first place. If you already have one, remember that, by definition, it is a "house cat." So confine it to the house and stock up on litter.

All right, so you bite the bullet and keep your cat indoors. What do you do about other cats that wander into your yard? You might try asking your local dog warden— oops, that should read "animal control officer"—to remove them.

That failing, there are several other methods you can try in order to discourage cats. Notice, I said "try." Cats being the cunning devils that they are, no method is a sure thing. Obviously, feeders can be placed high enough above the ground so that not even "a Michael Jordan of a cat" can reach them. However, if seeds spill onto the ground and attracts birds that like to feed there, they could be vulnerable to a feline assault. Moreover, perhaps you want to entice ground-feeding birds. How, then, do you keep cats at bay?

One frequently recommended tactic is to place feeders several feet away from vegetative cover that can conceal a cat while it creeps close enough for its final rush. An appropriate distance is ten feet. This helps, but there are two sides to the coin as far as cover is concerned. Small birds can quickly find refuge from hawks in vegetation growing near a feeder. I have several feeders hanging from a crab apple tree in my side yard. Juncos, white-throated sparrows, and cardinals regularly gather beneath them to pick up fallen seed. About four feet distant is a large rhododendron bush. When they perceive danger, the ground foragers explode into flight like a starburst, and unfailingly, most of them scoot for the shelter of the rhododendron.

Some people surround the ground where birds feed with a chicken wire fence. Such a fence does ward off cats, although it leaves something to be desired aesthetically. I suspect, moreover, that a barrier of this sort may inhibit the flight response of birds. Often when a group of birds is alarmed, they simultaneously disperse, flying in a dizzying number of direction, a behavior that confuses predators. A fence barrier tends to channel fleeing birds upward in the same direction—keeping them safe from a marauding cat, all right, but bunching them up and perhaps making them more vulnerable to attack by a hawk.

Hawkeyes

There is a touch of black humor that periodically makes the rounds among birders. The proverbial little old lady in tennis shoes visits a rather crusty friend who has set up a feeding station to attract songbirds. "That's nice," she says, "what kind of birds are you feeding?" "Hawks," is the reply.

Some of the worst enemies of feeder birds are other birds, notably hawks. A feeder can be a lunch counter not only for songbirds but also for the hawks that prey on them. Some hawks learn to regularly check out feeders for a quick, easy hit. The worst offenders at feeders are the sharp-shinned hawk and the Cooper's hawk. which feed mostly on smaller birds. The sharp-shinned is ten-and a-half inches in length, the Cooper's five inches longer. Both belong to a group of hawks known as accipiters. The accipiters have long tails and short wings, allowing them superior maneuverability in flight and enabling them to weave their way through the trees of the open woodlands they prefer to inhabit.

The Cooper's hawk is a secretive hunter. It perches concealed among branches, sometimes waiting patiently for hours, until an unwary bird comes in range. If the intended victim remains out of reach, the hawk may fly silently through the trees and take up a perch in a more advantageous position. I have observed the hunting behavior of the Cooper's hawk on many occasions. In back of my home are pens where I raise quail, pheasants, and a handful of guinea fowl. The pens, framed with wood and covered by netting, are located where woods interface with my lawn, and so are situated in the type of forest edge where Cooper's hawks like to hunt.

I first became aware that a Cooper's hawk had discovered my pens—and had a quail dinner on its mind—during my second summer as a game bird breeder. One afternoon in early summer, I heard a loud whirring of wings as my quail erupted into panicked flight within their pen. I went to the pen, expecting to see a prowling dog or cat. But I saw neither. Then, on the periphery of my vision, I saw a

movement in the canopy of trees that grow behind the pen. Silent as a shadow, a Cooper's hawk, which I had disturbed from its perch, winged away through the branches. It did not go far, but settled on a limb about fifty yards away. There it waited until I shouted and loudly clapped my hands, causing it to head for the deep woods. For the rest of the summer, the hawk—I assume it was the same one—perched above the pen almost every day. By the end of the summer, it must have been one frustrated creature. For all its patience, the hawk could not get at the quail because of the protective netting, although it probably made fast work of a handful that escaped from the pen. Cooper's hawks, by the way, never pass up the chance to grab a bird that is weak or sick. They have been observed catching feeder birds that have been knocked unconscious by collision with a window.

Sharp-shinned hawks hunt more actively than the Cooper's. They cruise, sometimes less than six feet from the ground, a behavior I witnessed literally about ten minutes before I wrote this section. I decided to take a break and go to our town's branch post office to pick up my mail. As I steered my truck out of my driveway, I spied a blue-gray form flitting out of the woods. Talk about coincidence. It was a sharp-shinned hawk. With powerful wing beats, it flew straight down the road, directly in front of me, for about fifty yards, then veered back into the trees. At no time was that bird more than a yard above the road's surface.

A week or so later, I had another encounter with a sharp-shinned hawk that made me wonder if the local population of the species had figured out I was writing about them and decided to strut their stuff. I was typing away on my computer keyboard when I heard a batch of blue jays sounding frantic alarm calls in the backyard, so I looked out the window. Next to a spruce tree, about thirty feet away, a sharp-shinned hawk had fastened its talons into a blue jay and pinned it to the ground. With wings and tail spread wide, the hawk bore down on its prey and appeared to hook its beak into the jay's neck. While the other jays screamed in outrage from within the boughs of the spruce, the hawk lifted off heavily, barely getting off the ground with the jay. Clearly, it was a difficult task, because the jay's body was almost the same size as the hawk's. The hawk flew for several feet across the lawn, so low that the jay almost brushed the grass, and disappeared behind another, larger spruce. I decided to remain at my computer rather than go outside and poke around, because I didn't want to chase the hawk from its meal, fairly earned.

Sharp-shinned hawks usually pluck birds off the

ground or out of trees, but they also bring them down out of the air. When pursuing a bird, the sharp-shinned stays right on its prey's tail, banking and turning like a fighter aircraft locked on target. Occasionally, however, the sharp-shinned will take a cue from the Cooper's and wait under cover for a bird to come near. I have seen one sitting within a fire bush that grows in the middle of my backyard, eyeing birds at a feeder twenty feet away.

"Sharpies," as birders often call them, can be persistent. A friend of mine has a feeder hanging over a deck outside the back door of her home. Approximately four feet from the feeder is a holly bush, and a few yards beyond the bush stands a small white birch tree. One summer day, she noticed a sharp-shinned hawk perching in the birch, eyeing a batch of songbirds gathered around the feeder. After several minutes, the sharpie launched a foray, but the songbirds all escaped into the recesses of the holly. The hawk then returned to the birch, from which it kept the bush under surveillance. Periodically, it made a pass at the holly, as if trying to roust the birds out of their shelter. Day after day, the hawk returned, often repeating the ritual for hours at a time. So intent was the hawk on its deadly game that it regularly ignored my friend's approach, even when she came within an arm's length of the birch.

My friend never witnessed a successful attack by the hawk, proof that protective cover near a feeder can be a useful deterrent against winged predators. Of course, bushes that shelter songbirds also may offer concealment to cats. An alternative that sometimes works when a hawk starts showing up around a feeder is to put temporary cover, such as an old Christmas tree or a heap of brush, nearby. Once the hawk becomes discouraged and moves to more productive hunting grounds, the cover can be removed.

It may sound a trifle heartless, but even if a hawk lunches on a bird or two, the situation is not all that bad. You will have the opportunity to see hawks up close. Besides, they have to eat, too.

Above all, remember that if you do any physical harm to a hawk—or any other bird of prey—you are violating federal wildlife law. Special agents of the United States Fish and Wildlife Service take a dim view of people who perpetrate wildlife crimes.

Bandits

There are a number of wild mammals that are prone to raid bird feeders. The most notable of these backyard bandits are arboreal squirrels, such as the gray squirrel and fox squirrel. (If you live in an area that lacks woodlands, tree squirrels obviously will not be around to trouble your feeders.) Once squirrels locate a feeder, they will do their darnedest to take their share of its bounty.

Outwitting squirrels at a feeder is a daunting proposition because they are remarkably brainy. Another friend of mine witnessed a demonstration of how astonishingly clever a squirrel can be if it hungers for the contents of a feeder. He happened to be looking at a suet cake that he had suspended from a slender branch by a short string. As he watched, a squirrel crept out on the branch, reached down, took the cake, and ate it. So he set out another cake, this time lengthening the string beyond the reach of the squirrel. The squirrel reappeared, drew up a portion of the string in its paws, and "with great deliberation," my friend observed, wrapped it around the branch three times. That trick brought the suet within reach, and the squirrel polished it off.

I find that suspending feeders about four or five feet down from branches and about six feet above the ground usually prevents squirrels from gaining access to them. However, I may be luckier than most. One of the reasons they create few problems for me is that they seem content to eat spillage off the ground. Diverting squirrels to a food source other than a bird feeder is, in fact, a workable alternative to waging a constant battle of wits with them. Some

people buy them off with cracked corn—cheaper than regular birdseed—placed in a bucket or on a tray set on the ground. You can also make a squirrel feeder by driving a large nail through a small board and mounting it, with the pointed end of the nail upward, on a low post. Then impale an ear of corn on the nail; the board will serve as a platform on which the squirrel can sit while eating the kernels of corn.

Several types of squirrel baffles that can be readily purchased work quite well. These devices, made of metal or plastic and usually shaped like cones or bowls, are placed over the string or wire on which the feeder is suspended or over the pole on which it is mounted. They are designed to block a squirrel's progress toward the feeder. Some feeders come equipped with baffles, which also help guard against cats and raccoons.

Raccoons can be much more of a problem than squirrels because when they raid a feeder, they may knock it down or tear it up—and since they are real trenchermen, they seldom stop eating until the seed runs out. Worse yet, in some parts of the country, rabies is prevalent among raccoons, so their presence certainly should not be encouraged. Note that if a raccoon is hanging out in your neighborhood, suet will draw it like a magnet draws iron filings. In such a case, it might be a good idea to forgo suet.

Once a raccoon sets its sights on your feeder it's crunch time. If you prefer to hang the feeder from a tree, suspend it from a branch that is too slender to carry the weight of a raccoon. This tactic can be fruitful but it has its disadvantages. You may have to use a smaller feeder than you might prefer, so you will have to fill it more frequently. Moreover, a raccoon may simply break the branch and consume the contents of the feeder on the ground.

Raccoons are such adept climbers that they often shinny up poles on which feeders are mounted. Some people coat feeder poles with automotive grease to thwart them. This has worked for me, but the pole has to be recoated regularly. The United States Fish and Wildlife Service recommends lathering poles with a mixture of petroleum jelly and hot pepper.

I have found that the best way to keep raccoons from

Protecting Birdhouses

The contents of birdhouses are a tempting target for animals that number among the backyard bandits. Red squirrels slip into a birdhouse through the entrance hole—they chew around the hole if it is too small—and feast on eggs and nestlings. Raccoons and cats will try to reach into the house and scoop out young—as well as adults that may be roosting for the night. Opossums sometimes take this approach, too. By itself, the three-quarter-inch wall around the entrance hole of a typical standard birdhouse is not thick enough to keep out a questing paw. However, doubling the thickness of the wood around the hole will do the trick. Nail a rectangular block of wood, three-quarters-of-an-inch thick, over the hole area. Of course, you must cut a hole in the block the same size as the entrance. A roof angled downward toward the front of the house with a three-inch overhang can also help discourage predators. As is the case with feeders, pole-mounted houses can be protected by baffles and grease.

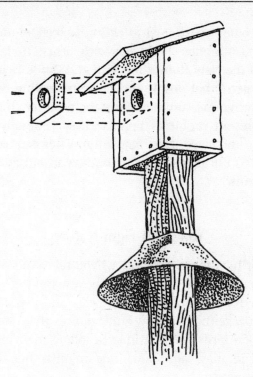

climbing posts or poles is to use a metal baffle especially designed for use against them. The baffle resembles a stovepipe, is capped at the top—with a hole to permit insertion of the pole—and open at the bottom, and is held in place by setscrews. Such baffles guard against squirrels as well as raccoons. In the long run, if raccoons persist in their unwanted visitations, it is probably best to contact a conservation officer or animal control official and have them removed.

If you live in black bear country, such as northern New England and the upper Midwest, be aware that bears sometimes become accustomed to eating at feeders during the spring and summer. Problems with bears, in fact, have prompted the New Hampshire Fish and Game Department to recommend that people abstain from feeding birds during the spring and summer. Once the weather chills, bears do not present problems because they generally stay in their dens and sleep. Dust baths and water can be used to attract birds during the warm months without attracting a hungry bruin.

You Can't Fight Nature

No matter how many precautions you take, you will never be able to make your feeders, nest boxes, and the birds that use them 100 percent safe from pests and predators. You can discourage them, surely, but creatures that raid feeders and prey on birds will continue to follow their instinct to survive. This may cause you some anguish, but they, too, are part of nature.

10

TWO DOZEN EXCELLENT BACKYARD BIRDS

Which are the most excellent backyard birds? The answer is very subjective. Some birds are valued for their song or their color, others for their interesting behavior, which is why species such as the evening grosbeak and cedar waxwing are on this list. Great backyard birds also include those you can count on to be around. Robins and chickadees are far from rare, but they enliven yards that birds requiring wild surroundings seldom, if ever, visit. As far as I am concerned, even house sparrows have a place on this list. If you live in the country and have the chance to attract bluebirds to a nest box, you will probably roust out house sparrows if they enter it. I have a friend who lives in a city, far from bluebirds and many of the other species that I can see in my yard. He put up a nest box and, within a day or so, house sparrows moved in, and he thoroughly enjoyed them. The fact of the matter is that any bird that visits your backyard and gives you enjoyment is excellent. (Unless noted, the birds shown in the illustrations are males.)

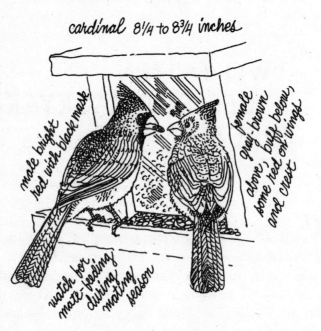

cardinal 8 1/4 to 8 3/4 inches

male bright red with black mask

female gray-brown above; buff below; some red on wings and crest

watch for mate-feeding during mating season

Northern Cardinal

When I was a boy a half century or so ago, the sight of a cardinal at a bird feeder in Connecticut was something to talk about. Today, cardinals are one of the most familiar feeder birds in my area and, although the gorgeous red of the male makes it one of the most colorful backyard birds, seeing one is no longer considered a memorable birding experience. Cardinals at the feeder are taken for granted.

The northern cardinal was once mainly a bird of the South, evidenced by the fact that it used to be called the "Virginia cardinal." However, it has extended its range as far north as southeastern Canada. Some ornithologists suspect that the expansion of the cardinal's range has occurred progressively, as young birds move into empty territories where food is available. If so, backyard feeders have undoubtedly played a role in extending the area over which this species is found. The cardinal lives from the East Coast into the plains states and edges into the Southwest as well. Cardinals do not migrate and will reside year-round in a place where they find the essentials of life.

Cardinals like habitat with at least some dense vegetation. Thickets, tangles of briars, shrubbery, and thorny shrubs such as barberries and hollies are used as sites for nests, which are usually no more than twelve feet above the ground. Cardinals particularly favor hedges and other low, thick vegetation if it is bordered by an open area, such as a lawn, near mixed woodland.

The extreme southwestern United States is the home of a close relative of the northern cardinal, the pyrrhuloxia. Like its cousin, this bird is crested. The male is grayish, with a red crest; the female is grayish brown. Its calls are very similar to those of the cardinal.

One reason cardinals have been able to spread so successfully is that they are very adaptable when it comes to diet. They feed on more than a hundred different kinds of seeds and fruits. Cultivated plants that will attract them include mulberry, blueberry, elderberry, dogwood, grapes, and Russian olive. Cardinals also consume insects. These may constitute almost a third of an adult bird's diet, so if you are a gardener they can be helpful birds to have around. They love sunflower seeds, but millet, corn, and a variety of other seeds will also keep them happy.

Once a pair of cardinals ties the knot, they isolate themselves within a breeding territory, which both sexes defend against other cardinals. Cardinals are a prime example of how bright color—at least in the red male—and loud song often go hand in hand with aggressive territorial defense. Unlike most songbird species, the female cardinal actually sings, although not as loudly as the male.

Cardinals build a cuplike nest placed between two and twelve feet from the ground. Yards with thickets and brush are attractive to cardinals when they are ready to start housekeeping. The female may lay two to six eggs, but usually three or four. Cardinals are among those birds that believe that from a reproductive standpoint, once is not enough. A pair may have more than one set of nestlings during a breeding season.

Mourning Dove

If Planned Parenthood ever decides to pick a bird as its emblem, it certainly will not be the mourning dove. Once male and female mourning doves pair up in the spring, they take the breeding season seriously. By late summer, they've often raised four broods. Most backyard birds have one brood per year. Some, such as cardinals, may raise two or three batches of young. But four? According to avian standards, that is mass production.

True, a female mourning dove lays a clutch of only two eggs, which is not a lot by songbird standards. Cardinals,

mourning dove -12 inches

nest of grass, twigs and weeds

dark spot on side of neck

as noted, lay from two to six eggs. But newly hatched mourning doves have an edge when it comes to survival—an immediate source of highly nutritious food. Both male and female doves produce a substance in their crops called "pigeon's milk," which in some ways is chemically similar to mammalian milk. The youngsters feed on this substance for the first few days of their lives. For the remainder of the two weeks that it takes them to fledge, the parents provide them with regurgitated food.

The mourning dove is cosmopolitan. Its range extends from coast to coast and from southern Canada to Central America. Except in the northernmost portion of its range, most mourning doves stay around all winter.

Mourning doves are not very choosy about habitat.

While they often concentrate around grain fields, much to the consternation of farmers, they readily adapt to open woods, evergreen groves, and suburban and urban yards.

Mourning doves feed on grain and on the seeds of grasses and weeds. They also eat berries from plants such as alder, holly, and serviceberry, which can be cultivated in the yard. Doves are avid feeder birds—tray feeders or the ground, please—and will eat a wide variety of seeds. These include the ever-popular sunflower, plus white proso millet, as well as milo, corn, and buckwheat, which are not favorites of most backyard birds.

Parent mourning doves have worked out a specific timetable for sharing incubation duties. The male sits on the eggs during the height of the day, and the female handles the job early in the morning and from late afternoon through the night.

For such attentive parents, mourning doves do not keep a tidy house. Their nest is built rather sloppily of twigs loosely woven into a platform. They make use of myriad nesting sites, including trees, shrubs, clusters of vines— even gutters and chimneys. Although the mourning dove nest may be as much as fifty feet off the ground, it is usually lower, between five and twenty-five feet up.

The mourning dove gets its name from its call—a melancholy "coo" followed by three more "coos," lower in tone. I find the sound peaceful, but other people think of it as mournful. Although the dove is a symbol of peace, the mourning dove does not live up to its reputation in that respect. It can be rather feisty and will sometimes bully smaller birds away from a feeding station. In many states within its range, the mourning dove is a popular game bird.

rufous-sided towhee – 7½ to 8½ inches

red eye on some

a ground feeder somewhat similar to a robin but, thinner, female has brown head, back, wings and tail (black on male)

white belly and rust-colored sides on both

white tail stripe

Rufous-Sided Towhee

A rufous-sided towhee hopping around the ground acts like a bird that is unsure of which direction it wants to travel. The towhee finds its food in leaf litter, which it scratches up by hopping, head down and tail up, forward and backward. A hungry towhee looks like a wind-up toy as it incessantly jumps back and forth. Especially if the litter is dry, this process makes so much noise that a towhee can sound almost like a bull moose crashing through the brush. Well, maybe not quite, but more than one person has mistaken the rustling of a towhee for a deer pussyfooting through the woods.

Oddly, even though the rufous-sided towhee can be found from coast to coast—year-round in many areas—some people refer to it as the eastern towhee. Presumably, the "eastern" designation is used to distinguish this towhee from three other species of towhee found only in the western states. The green-tailed towhee inhabits much of the region west of the Rocky Mountains. The brown towhee lives along the West Coast and in parts of the Southwest. Albert's towhee is also a southwestern bird.

Towhees are primarily birds of deciduous woodlands. A yard that is bordered by trees and brush is likely to have towhees in its vicinity. The best feeder placement is at the edge of the lawn, close to the woods.

Due to their feeding habits, towhees often stay out of sight beneath underbrush. However, their vocalizations often reveal their presence when they are not visible. One call of the rufous-sided towhee sounds likes its name: "towhee." Another is "chewink." The song is best described as "drink-your-tea."

The rufous-sided towhee pretty much splits its food consumption between plant materials and small animals, although in winter, when insects are sparse, plant matter predominates. Towhees eat a wide variety of grass seeds as well as several sorts of berries. Their animal food includes insects such as beetles, ants, crickets, and caterpillars, as well as spiders and even small lizards. Towhees will come to low feeders or, better yet, feed on the ground. They will take cracked corn as well as sunflower seeds.

The nest of the towhee, made of grasses, leaves, and bits of bark, is placed on the ground in a spot hidden by brush. The female usually lays between two and six eggs.

blue jay
11 to 12 inches

blue back and top of head

white bars

white belly

stores acorns and nuts for winter use

Blue Jay

Blue jays often are described as being rascally, bold, aggressive, rowdy, and pushy. Rightly so. Yet they are among the most beautifully colored of any North American songbirds. Why don't they get more credit for their beauty? Precisely because they are rascally, bold, aggressive, rowdy, and pushy. In addition, they occasionally eat the eggs and nestlings of other songbirds, and they are as common as old shoes throughout most of the country. They inhabit virtually all of the eastern United States, the Great Plains, and much of Canada. If blue jays were rare, I believe we would treasure them despite some of their less-desirable habits.

If you are among those who dislike having jays at your feeder because they scare off many other birds, try being objective about this extraordinary species. Besides its gorgeous plumage, it acts with uncanny intelligence. Blue jays intuitively plan ahead, and are known to bury acorns and seeds in the ground for use in lean times. Listing the number of calls made by the blue jay would probably take this entire page. They have several of their own and they are superb mimics. A blue jay can imitate the scream of a red-shouldered hawk so well that it's very difficult to distinguish it from the real thing. I know that for a fact. When red-shouldered hawks and jays are in my yard at the same time, I have to work hard to figure out which call comes from which bird.

Despite the fact that blue jays are backyard bird toughs, they sometimes do their avian neighbors a service. Let a predator come prowling about and blue jays will erupt in a chorus of raucous alarm calls that sound like "thief, thief, thief." In the blue jay's case, calling an interloper a thief is like the pot blackguarding the kettle. But the alarm does put other birds on the alert—and probably saves the lives of some.

If you have a yard with even a few trees or bushes, chances are good that it may interest blue jays when the time comes to nest. They build a rather large cup of twigs, bark, leaves, and other assorted plant materials. Surprisingly for such rough-edged birds, parent blue jays do their utmost to make the inside of the nest soft and comfy for their young by lining it with grass and fine rootlets. Usually, the female lays four or five eggs within the nest, which is between five and fifty feet above the ground. The parental devotion of the blue jay extends to a fiery defense of its nest. They will buzz and harass any intruder. When I was a child, our family cat climbed high into a shagbark hickory tree that held a blue jay nest. The cat had, in effect, twisted the tail of the tiger. The two adult blue jays, screaming like banshees, dive-bombed the poor cat. Totally cowed, it took refuge in the crotch of a branch, put its back against the trunk, and hoped for the best. Having stalled the advance of the feline, the blue jays backed off a bit, allowing the terrified cat to scramble out of the branches and down the trunk to safety.

Blue jays are real chowhounds. They are not a whit discriminating about what they eat. Snail or salamander? Insects? A young mouse? All are fare for the blue jay. However, seeds, berries, and other plant materials are their mainstay. So is just about anything you would put in your feeder.

Blue jays will never be wimps. You may not want them in your backyard. I do.

Black-Capped Chickadee

Here is the quintessential feeder bird; it's around all year and abundant in the backyard, even in many urban areas. The black-capped chickadee lives throughout most of North America north to Alaska. Several closely allied chickadees—so similar that their plumages and behaviors are almost identical—overlap portions of the black-capped chickadee's range. The Carolina chickadee lives from New

black-capped chickadee
4½ to 5½ inches

black cap
and bib,
gray wings
and back

some white
on wings

often feeds
upside down

Jersey south to Florida and as far west as Kansas. The mountain chickadee is a bird of the Rockies, the Sierra Nevada, and the Pacific Coastal Range. The Mexican chickadee edges into Arizona and New Mexico from south of the border. The boreal chickadee inhabits the northern coniferous forest of Canada and Alaska. Along the rim of the West Coast lives yet another member of the clan, the chestnut-backed chickadee.

Chickadees are active, engaging little birds that readily come to feeders. Some books describe them as "tame," but to be more precise, they are not afraid to come close to people. They can be conditioned to take food right out of the hand. If you stand quietly near a feeder with a hand extended and filled with sunflower seeds, and have the patience to do it for an hour or so over the space of several days, you can teach chickadees this behavior. I knew a guy who actually trained them to sit on his head. He always wore a hat.

Except during the nesting season, chickadees move around in small groups in search of food. Their liking for sunflower seeds belies the fact that, especially in summer, they are largely insect eaters. Beetles, caterpillars, and ants are taken with relish. Chickadees often perform acrobatics as they pick insect eggs and larvae from the bark of trees, hanging upside down if they must to get at their prey. As the insect supply dwindles in winter, plant foods become more important to chickadees and constitute up to half of their intake. They like pine and hemlock seeds, as well as berries, including those of poison ivy. (Many birds and mammals can eat poison ivy berries without suffering ill effects.) Virtually any type of feeder stocked with sunflower will attract them.

When the time to nest arrives, chickadees may appropriate an abandoned woodpecker hole, use a cavity in a tree, or excavate their own hole out of rotting wood. They usually choose a nest site no more than ten feet above the ground. Because of their hole-nesting habit, they are prime candidates for nesting boxes. The adults line the bottom of their nesting cavity with soft material, including moss, plant fibers, and feathers. The female lays six to eight eggs and incubates them for almost two weeks.

Tufted Titmouse

The tufted titmouse is a close relative of the chickadee and, like it, is a common backyard bird in many areas. This little

tufted titmouse - 6 to 6½ inches

gray back and crest

some black on forehead

buff flanks

pale gray belly

bird inhabits the eastern half of the country. In the western states, the most widespread titmouse is the plain titmouse, which ranges from western Wyoming to the Pacific Coast. The name of the plain titmouse has nothing to do with its habitat, because it is found in mountains rather than on the flatlands. Like the tufted titmouse, which it resembles, it is a plain-colored bird.

A wide variety of wooded habitats suit the tufted titmouse, including forests of coniferous or deciduous trees, swamps, orchards, parks, and suburban backyards. Tufted titmice are likely to be seen year-round in a yard or neighborhood that contains a fair number of trees. These birds are among the species that have extended their range considerably since the 1940s, when they were seldom seen in the northern part of the territory they now regularly inhabit.

Gray above and soft white below, the titmouse is not a

splashy bird in terms of color. However, if you look at a titmouse closely, you will see a buff-red patch under its wings and along its flanks. And if you look at one very, very closely, you will notice what may be its most attractive feature—bright, shiny black eyes.

Tufted titmice are noisy little creatures that seem to be talking constantly to one another. Their spring and summer call is a loud whistle, best described as "peto, peto, peto," or "peter, peter, peter." Take your pick. The call most often heard in the winter is nasal and scolding. A flock of calling tufted titmice can set the winter woods a-buzzing.

The winter tufted titmouse flock is generally made up of an adult pair and their young of the year, although sometimes chickadees mix in. Tufted titmice range farther afield during the winter than at other times of year, sometimes covering more than fifteen acres as they search for food.

During the winter, at least 70 percent of the tufted titmouse's diet consists of plant foods. Acorns, hickory nuts, seeds of various types, and berries are among its staples. Sunflower seeds, peanuts, and suet will attract them to feeders. Tufted titmice switch mainly to insects as food during the summer, although they will continue to visit feeders.

Watching a tufted titmouse break the shells of sunflower seeds and eat them is a treat because of the neat, methodical way in which the bird feeds. First it takes a single seed in its bill. It may fly to another perch or, if the perch on the feeder is large enough, remain there. Next, the titmouse transfers the seed to its feet and holds it down so that it can break it open with its bill. The bird accomplishes this with a series of sharp blows. Tufted titmice regularly perform this behavior at a small plastic window feeder outside my kitchen. Even while indoors, I can hear the regular tapping as they break open seeds—in effect, they tap outside my chamber door.

In the late winter, flocks of tufted titmice begin to disintegrate as males prepare to establish breeding territories in the spring. As the flock society falls apart, its members become quite testy toward one another. The flock flies erratically through the trees as the birds scold and chase one another energetically.

Male and female titmice are pretty faithful to each other as birds go, and often pair for life. The nesting habits of the titmouse resemble those of black-capped chickadees. A woodpecker hole or other cavity in a tree or stump serves as shelter for the nest, but titmice will also use nesting boxes. Once settled, the female usually lays five or six eggs.

White-Breasted Nuthatch

It might appear that a bird that feeds while perched upside down has something of a gravity problem, but there is a very definite method behind the apparent madness of the white-breasted nuthatch. The nuthatch competes with woodpeckers as well as brown creepers, small, inconspicuous birds, that exhibit the similar feeding behavior of picking insects out of bark while clinging to tree trunks and branches. Woodpeckers and creepers work their way up a tree, while the white-breasted nuthatch—and its nuthatch relatives—descend headfirst. Crafty. The nuthatch is able to probe for insects in cracks and crevices that its competition, oppositely positioned, tends to miss.

white-breasted nuthatch 5 to 6 inches

blue-gray back and wings

black cap on male—blue-gray on female

The white-breasted nuthatch, which is the largest nuthatch species in size, has a year-round range comprising most of the United States and a large portion of Canada. The red-breasted nuthatch is found from coast to coast in the United States and edges north into the Canadian forests during the nesting season. There are two other nuthatches in North America: the brown nuthatch of the southeastern states and the pygmy nuthatch of the western mountains. All nuthatches basically favor woodlands containing nut-bearing trees, such as oaks and beeches, and can be drawn to backyards with large trees.

Although insects comprise the bulk of a nuthatch's diet, it also eats seeds, acorns, and beechnuts. Its name, in fact, comes from the way it opens up a nut or a seed. Nuthatches wedge nuts and seeds into crevices in bark and bang away at them with their strong bills. Nuthatches also store food in crevices for later consumption. They will visit feeders, especially for sunflower seeds and suet.

The most common year-round call of the nuthatch is a nasal, low "yank, yank." A nuthatch couple uses it to keep in touch with each other. Nuthatches also use this call when having territorial disputes. When arguing over turf, nuthatches square off on a tree trunk, feathers ruffled and wings slightly parted. They circle, dart, and parry until one of them tires of the affair and departs.

Like titmice, nuthatches generally pair for life. They begin breeding in late winter or early spring and nest in tree cavities, including old woodpecker holes. Sometimes they dig their own holes in soft, decaying wood. They will use nest boxes, but these must be stationed high up in a tree, since nuthatches nest between fifteen and fifty feet above ground level. Grasses, fur, shreds of bark, rootlets, and other soft materials are used by the female to line the nesting cavity where she lays five to ten eggs.

Eastern Phoebe

I have a particular liking for the eastern phoebe because it helps me catch trout. Phoebes migrating from the southern states arrive in my area during the month of April, when the trout season opens. Some years ago I learned that the fact they often catch insects off the water is a clue to where the trout are lurking.

The eastern phoebe—its western relatives are the black phoebe and Say's phoebe—belongs to the family of birds

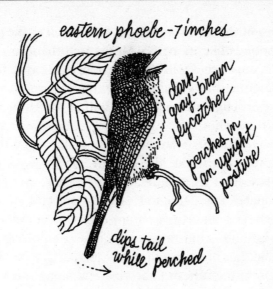

eastern phoebe - 7 inches

dark gray-brown flycatcher

perches in an upright posture

dips tail while perched

known as flycatchers. That's what they do. They perch in trees and scan their surroundings for flies and other winged insects. When they see prey, they dart after it and snap it up. Most flycatchers snap up their prey in midair. Some, however, including the eastern phoebe, snatch emerging caddisflies and mayflies off the surface of water so deftly they hardly cause a ripple.

During the spring breeding period, phoebes often congregate near streams. A smart move on their part. Aquatic nymphs that are changing into winged adults provide them with a constant supply of food for themselves and their young. From their perches, the phoebes flutter to the water and pick off their targets. Unlike swallows, which skim over the water, phoebes strike directly. Chances are, if phoebes are taking flies from above, trout are doing the same from below. When I am working a stream during the early part of trout season, I listen for the call of the phoebe, which sounds like its name. More often than not, a large grouping of phoebes will show me where to cast a fly.

During the spring and summer, the eastern phoebe can be found throughout the eastern half of the United States and northwest into the Mackenzie region of Canada. Although its underparts are brownish white with a touch of yellow, from a distance the eastern phoebe looks grayish black because of its dark head, wings, back, and tail. The black phoebe closely resembles the eastern bird but it has a much whiter belly. It lives from central California to the Southwest and is not migratory. The Say's phoebe is dark topside but has brownish orange underparts. It can be seen year-round in Southern California and along the Mexican border through Texas and migrates north as far as Alaska in the spring. The eastern and black phoebes use a variety of habitats, including woodlands, farmlands, suburbs, and even urban areas. The Say's phoebe prefers open areas and is often found in arid countryside.

All phoebes build their nests on ledges and on man-made structures, such as the sides of buildings. They will come to an artificial nesting platform. The females usually lay between two and eight eggs.

American Robin

The American robin illustrates that, once a fallacy takes hold, it becomes fact. First of all, the American robin is not a real robin. The genuine article is a European bird, which, like the American robin, has an orange-red breast. The Eu-

american robin
9½ to 10½ inches

also eats insects
and berries as
well as worms

ropean bird, however, deserves the name "robin," with no adjective preceding it. The American robin was misnamed by early British colonists who noticed its resemblance to the robin they had left behind in the Old World. (They made similar mistakes with other American creatures. For example, they described the skunk as a "polecat." Although it is related to the European polecat—both are members of the weasel family—the skunk is an entirely different critter.) Similarly, the American robin, like the robin, is a thrush, but the two are not all that closely related. Much closer kin to the American robin is another European bird called the "blackbird" in keeping with its coloring. Note, by the way, that it is in no way a member of the group we call "blackbirds" on this side of the Pond.

And, to confuse matters more, the American robin some-times wanders to Europe, where it has been reported as far from its normal range as the former Yugoslavia.

As its name implies, this bird is a real American. Its range includes all of North America, south of the Arctic tundra, and extends as far south as Central America. Rob-ins leave the northern half of their range in the fall, but some can be found in northern states all winter. Even on a cold winter day in southern New England, for example, it is not uncommon to see a robin poking about in a thicket looking for berries. That is not to say that particular bird is a year-round resident. It could very well be a bird from Maine or Canada that has shifted southward. All of which brings up another misconception. In areas such as mine, the robin, which people like to view as a harbinger of spring, may have been around all winter.

Although the American robin symbolizes the saying "the early bird gets the worm," it does not live exclusively on worms year-round. Worms are admittedly a major food during the spring and summer, but a robin patrolling your lawn may also be eating grubs, since robins consume a large variety of insects. As fall approaches, berries and fruit become a much greater portion of the robin's diet. During the winter, when worms are hard to come by in many areas inhabited by robins, fruits and berries are a mainstay. Be-cause of the robin's fondness for berries, people who grow crops such as blueberries do not share the feelings the rest of us have for the Redbreast. In parts of Maine, where blue-berries are a staple crop, robins are about as welcome as influenza.

Although robins are among the most familiar backyard birds, they generally are not considered feeder birds, since they are not seed eaters. Sometimes, however, they will come to feeders at which berries or pieces of chopped fruit are offered, and they will respond well to mealworms.

Robins will nest in a yard that has trees and shrubs with thick foliage and plenty of branches. They build their nests, of twigs and grasses cemented with mud, on horizontal branches. Female robins lay three to six eggs, with four as the average.

slate-colored
dark-eyed junco — 6 inches
dark gray with white belly
light bill
dark tail with conspicuous white edge

Dark-Eyed Junco

Taxonomists are academicians who earn their living by naming organisms, including birds. They give each bird two types of name. One is its "scientific" name, which is in Latin so, presumably, scientists can understand it. The other is its "common" name, the designated term generally used by average folk to identify a species.

Whether scientific or common, each name refers to a particular species. This system would actually be rather neat but for the fickle nature of taxonomists. They continually change the names and relationships of species, and in recent years, they seem to be doing it more frequently, largely based on DNA studies of genetic relationships and the professed desire to create names that are consistent on an international basis. For example, they will confer upon a particular beast the honor of being a species unto itself. Ten years later they strip the poor critter of its name and unique status, then lump it with some relative and proclaim that they now are one. Over the years, taxonomists have probably added and subtracted more species from the list of living things than you have written entries in your checkbook.

Consider the junco, which, during the winter, descends from mountain heights and Canadian forests to virtually all of the lower 48 states and is the most widespread bird at North American feeders. For years, birders dutifully accepted the word of taxonomists that there were five different species of juncos whose cumulative range included just about all of North America above Mexico. Pick up any old, dog-eared field guide to see all five species on parade: the slate-colored junco, the Oregon junco, the white-winged junco, the pink-sided junco, and the gray-headed junco. Their general coloration is gray to grayish brown above and white below, but the fact that each type of junco had a dab or two of coloration that the others did not was used by the taxonomists to justify breaking them down into individual species. In reality, however, birders had taken a juicy worm tossed out by the taxonomists. They let birders play with the bait for a while, then—whammo—they set the hook.

Suddenly, field guides by the millions were out of date because the taxonomists changed their minds about juncos. The five had become one species, but with a new name—the dark-eyed junco, undoubtedly because they all have dark eyes. Birders scratched their heads, wrestled with the new name, and now wait for the taxonomists' latest surprise. It could come from south of the Mexican border. There lives a junco with yellow eyes that the taxonomists deem to be a species of its own, separate from the dark-eyed junco. Understandably, it is called the "yellow-eyed junco." Somewhere there may be a coven of taxonomists who are seeking a way to combine the dark-eyed and yellow-eyed juncos into one species with a new name, perhaps just plain "junco," or to affirm that there are six species of juncos after all—for now, at least.

Whatever you want to call them, juncos are common birds in backyards and brushy fields during the winter, when they migrate south from the boreal forest of Canada and Alaska. You won't find them on the tundra. They also reside year-round in higher elevations of the mountain West, the Appalachians, and northern New England. They arrive in flocks during late fall and are among the earliest birds to head north in the spring. Juncos like to feed on the ground, where they forage for weed and grass seeds. Spillover from hanging sunflower feeders attracts them, and they quickly adapt to low tray feeders.

Juncos nest in coniferous and mixed forests, often along tree lines next to clearings, lakes, and streams. Their nests are on or near the ground, often hidden among the roots of fallen trees, under logs, or on rocky ledges. The female lays four to five eggs.

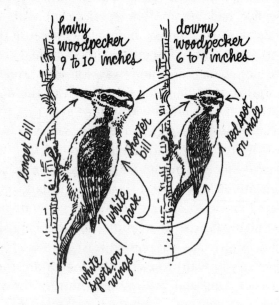

hairy woodpecker 9 to 10 inches

downy woodpecker 6 to 7 inches

longer bill

shorter bill

red spot on male

white back

white spots on wings

Hairy Woodpecker

Despite its name, the hairy woodpecker isn't a freak among birds. It has feathers, just like all other birds. Like its smaller look-alike, the downy woodpecker, the hairy has a range that rivals that of the American robin—just about all of North America south of the Arctic tundra. Unlike the robin, these two woodpeckers are permanent residents wherever they live. Wooded areas are their preferred habitat, but they also frequent plains and deserts where they can find stands and groves of trees.

Beginning birders may tend to confuse the two species, both of which are predominately black and white in color, with a red patch on the nape of the neck distinguishing males from females. The hairy, however, is larger, and has a longer bill.

These woodpeckers feed mostly on insects, especially those that bore into wood. They also will sample berries and seeds. They will come to a sunflower feeder with regularity, especially if it is suspended from a tree on which they hunt insects, and suet is a sure draw. If you have large, mature trees in your yard, you may discover that you have hairy woodpeckers for permanent neighbors.

Woodpeckers have several interesting adaptations for their way of life. The skull of a woodpecker is thicker than that of most other birds, which protects the brain from the jarring impact of a woodpecker's bill when it hammers into the wood of trees. Further protection comes from a membrane between the skull and the brain and a bone around the delicate optic nerve.

Since a woodpecker feeds while clinging to the surface of a limb or trunk, it needs toes that can anchor it firmly in place as it searches for insects. Most birds have three toes facing forward and one that faces backward; the woodpecker's arrangement is two in front, two behind. Long, stiff feathers in the woodpecker's tail serve as a prop against the surface beneath the bird.

Like most other woodpeckers, the hairy species nests in a cavity that it digs in a tree at up to thirty feet above ground level. Both male and female carry on the excavation. Wood chips that fall into the hole serve as bedding for the nest. These woodpeckers also use nest boxes. After the eggs are laid—a clutch usually has four of them—the parents share the incubation duties.

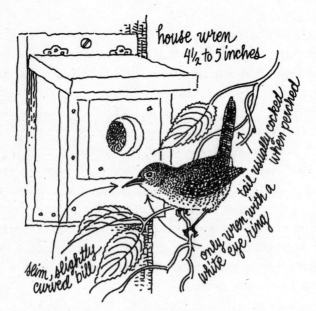

house wren
4½ to 5 inches

tail usually cocked
when perched

only wren with a
white eye ring

slim, slightly
curved bill

House Wren

The house wren is another of those birds that ranges over a wide geographical area. During the spring and summer, it nests from coast to coast and north into central Canada. Although they cannot be considered urban birds, house wrens adapt well to backyards with vegetation and, especially, gardens. They should be welcomed to the garden because they are voracious insect eaters.

People find house wrens cute and their bubbling song uplifting. Other hole-nesting birds do not view them as so endearing. Male house wrens sometimes try to drive other cavity-nesting species from their holes and will even destroy their nests, eggs, or young.

The house wren is most common in the eastern part of its range. Another abundant eastern wren is the Carolina wren. It is larger than the house wren and has a distinct white streak resembling an eyebrow over its eye. While the overall plumage of the house wren is dull grayish brown, the Carolina wren's plumage has a rusty cast. Another small wren, the winter wren, breeds across central Canada. It migrates to the lower forty-eight states during the winter, when its range overlaps that of the house wren in the eastern part of the country. There are some similarities between the two, although the winter wren is smaller and its plumage is not as bland as that of the house wren. Its tail is also stubbier. The extreme northern portion of the house wren's breeding range coincides partly with the southern extreme of the winter wren's spring and summer range.

Western wrens include the cactus wren (the largest wren in North America), the rock wren, and the canyon wren. The cactus wren, more than six inches long, is a bird of the southwestern deserts and is commonly found among cacti and desert shrubs such as mesquite, especially near streams or dry streambeds. Like house wrens, cactus wrens also nest in suburban areas. The rock wren and canyon wren are widespread throughout the West within rugged, rocky areas.

House wrens frequently use nest boxes. They naturally nest in tree cavities. Male house wrens arrive on the nesting ground first and fill several holes with sticks and twigs. When the female arrives, she takes her pick of holes. She may toss out the sticks or leave them as a bed for her nest.

Once she chooses a nest site, the pair mates. The female incubates the eggs—up to an astonishing dozen of them in rare cases—while the male keeps her supplied with food.

evening grosbeak
8 inches

female—silver-gray with yellow cast

large white wing patches

male—dull yellow, dark head with yellow eyebrow stripe

white on tail

black and white wings

black tail

Evening Grosbeak

The evening grosbeak is a bird with pizazz. Noisy, robust and flashy, with males sporting plumage of yellow, black, and white, the evening grosbeak is gregarious, hanging out in large flocks even during nesting season, when most songbirds separate into pairs. Grosbeaks descend upon a feeder en masse, fluttering and calling with shrill, harsh chirps. They may not stay long, but while they're around they are a sight to behold. I consider any winter that evening grosbeaks visit my yard one to remember; I wish it happened more often.

Evening grosbeaks are among the birds of the northern coniferous and mixed forests that make irruptions, those unpredictable mass incursions south from their usual habitat. Even when not driven by a food supply crisis up north, their southward winter migrations are irregular. Lucky birders in the western states and across Canada can see evening grosbeaks year-round. During the winter, some grosbeaks edge south, and their periodic irruptions can take them as far as the Carolinas. Ornithologists believe they are extending their range—perhaps because of food they obtain from bird feeders—and that is definitely a welcome trend.

The diet of grosbeaks, like that of many other birds, changes seasonally. During the summer, when insects are abundant, evening grosbeaks feed on them to a large degree. Plant materials, including the seeds of maples, pines, spruces, and firs, plus many types of berries, are their mainstays the rest of the year. They usually remain in heavy forest unless tempted into the open by a feeder full of sunflower. Tray feeders, including those raised well above the ground, are most attractive to them, although they will also swarm around other varieties of feeders.

Male evening grosbeaks do not go a-courting outside of the flock to which they belong. Like fish in a school, the members of the flock that feed together breed together. The evening grosbeak builds a nest of materials such as twigs and mosses, sometimes placing it a hundred feet above the ground. The female lays from two to five eggs as a rule.

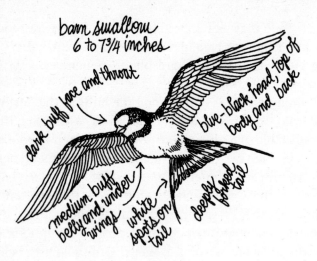

barn swallow
6 to 7¾ inches

dark buff face and throat

blue-black head, top of body and back

medium buff belly and under wings

white spots on tail

deeply forked tail

Barn Swallow

Barn swallows are true world citizens. They plaster their superbly engineered cups of mud or clay to ledges, cliffs, and buildings all across North America, Asia, and Europe, as well as in northern Africa. You will find them in places as remote from each other as Texas and Japan. When winter grips the Northern Hemisphere, they migrate as far south as New Guinea and South America. In North America, they range as far north as the tree line: although they do not like truly dense forest, they need trees about them.

As their name seems to imply, barn swallows like to live in the countryside rather than the city. Yet, I have seen them wing in by the thousands at dusk in downtown Bangkok, to settle shoulder-to-shoulder on utility wires, all eyes front in perfect formation as they roost for the night.

Most backyards, however, are visited by flocks of barn swallows as they gracefully pursue insects overhead, swooping and arcing in a stunning aerial ballet. From the ground, some types of swallows are difficult to distinguish from one another, especially since they are real blazers while on the wing. It is difficult to fix binoculars on a swallow when it is lusting after a juicy insect and in hot pursuit of its meal. Bank swallow? Cliff swallow? Both have short forked tails and white underparts and may be difficult to tell apart when glimpsed only fleetingly. The bank swallow has a brown collar, visible from down below, if there is time to see it. The barn swallow, on the other hand, is unmistakable. Its long forked tail is its trademark. No other North American swallow has a tail that is so deeply forked.

The bank swallow is another species found in North America, and has a global range that approximates the barn swallow's. Its breeding range also extends across Eurasia and includes northern Africa. In the United States, however, it does not breed in the southwestern or southeastern states.

All told, there are eight species of swallows that are North American nesters. Swallows spend more time on the wing than any other members of the family of perching birds, almost as much as the swifts, which, like swallows, catch insects in the air but belong to a family of their own. Even their courtship is carried on almost completely in the sky.

Can a barn swallow really be considered a backyard bird? It can if you have a barn or even an open shed on your property, because, assuming the proper habitat exists in your area, barn swallows may nest in these structures. Also, they qualify as backyard birds because they will use artificial nesting platforms. Their nest is a cup of mud, which they build pellet by pellet and line with soft materials such as feathers. The eggs laid by the female usually number between two and seven.

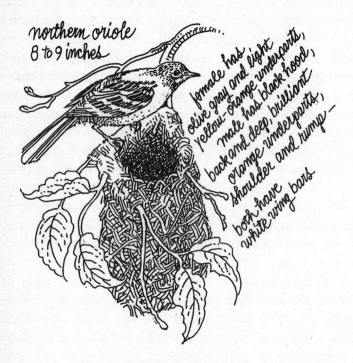

northern oriole
8 to 9 inches

female has light
olive gray and light
yellow-orange underparts,
male has black hood,
back and deep, brilliant
orange underparts,
shoulder and rump—
both have
white wing bars

Baltimore Oriole

The Baltimore oriole is another of those birds whose name is mired in confusion because it has been switched around by taxonomists. At one time, the Baltimore oriole, which lives mostly in the eastern half of North America, and the Bullock's oriole of the west were considered distinct species. But that all changed when taxonomists decided they were really two races of the same species, which was christened the "northern oriole." (The baseball team named after the Baltimore oriole paid no heed to the taxonomists and didn't change its name.) The designation "northern" was given to the bird because its nesting range extends into central Canada and no other North American oriole makes it that far north. During the fall, the oriole migrates south, from the coasts of the southeastern and Gulf states to South America. Birders became accustomed to thinking of both orioles as one species. However, in 1995, the situation suddenly changed as scientists decided they had been right in the first place. So it was back to Baltimore and Bullock's as two separate species.

Baltimore orioles eat a variety of fruits and insects as well as flower nectar. They can be attracted to feeders with the same nectar used for hummingbirds. Orioles also will come to a halved orange.

Beautiful birds with a pleasing song, Baltimore orioles nest in rural, suburban, and even some urban areas where shade trees are present. They usually stay away from dense forest, opting instead to nest in trees that are near openings or clearings. In my yard, they nest in a white oak standing adjacent to a weed field, which provides them with nesting materials.

The Baltimore oriole is famed for its elaborately woven nest that is shaped like a pouch and hangs from the end of a tree limb. Suspending a nest at the tip of a limb is a survival strategy for the young because the limb will not support the weight of potential predators, such as raccoons. Besides plant materials, orioles often weave string and hair into their nest, which is usually placed fairly high above the ground, most often between twenty-five and thirty feet, but sometimes considerably higher, which further discourages predators. Baltimore orioles lay from three to six eggs, with four being the usual number.

gray catbird
8½ to 9 inches

slim and
gray with black
cap

chestnut
under tail

Gray Catbird

People disagree considerably about the musical talents of the gray catbird. Some listeners consider the catbird to be a distinctly unmelodious creature and the sounds that it makes to be harsh, squeaky, or squealing. Others—I am one—enjoy listening to a catbird's complicated mix of musical phrases interspersed with the mewing sound that is responsible for its name. Either way, no one can dispute that the catbird sings with gusto, and once it starts, it hates to quit, sometimes continuing into the night—very unusual behavior for a songbird. The catbird does not require stands of large trees and can live quite happily among shrubbery, so it often enlivens with its songs yards that do not attract many other birds. Whether or not those songs are harmonious, at least the catbird brings bird music into yards that otherwise might be silent.

Catbirds have a wide range but are missing from some of the westernmost states. As summer fades, catbirds begin to migrate south, although some remain for the winter along the East and Gulf Coasts. The migrants spend the winter from the southern states to Central America.

Dense thickets of shrubs, even those less than six feet high, will attract catbirds. Undergrowth is a plus for them, especially if it is near plants that produce berries. If they find a suitable habitat, they tend to stick around a small area during their nesting season.

Catbirds feed on a combination of berries and insects, and also a few seeds. Plants that draw them—both for cover and food—include bittersweet, grapes, and honeysuckle. Although catbirds are not generally considered feeder birds, they can be enticed to a feeding station. Placed on a tray, chopped apples, raisins, and cherries will attract them.

The catbird is a relative of the mockingbird and the thrashers. Unlike them, however, catbirds are a peaceable species and not aggressive toward other birds. Along with their relatives, catbirds are solitary. They do not flock and only get together when couples join up for breeding and nesting.

The nest of the catbird is made of twigs, sticks, leaves, grasses, and weeds. From the outside it looks rather roughly built, but inside is a smooth cup carefully lined with soft materials such as rootlets, the bark of vines, and hair. Catbirds place their nests low to the ground—usually no more than fifteen feet up—within tangles of vines, shrubs, and low trees. They lay from two to six eggs and may have two broods a year.

Song Sparrow

Like the catbird, the song sparrow brings great cheer to the yards that it visits. From its perch, sometimes on the top-most spire of a tree, the male sings incessantly, especially

song sparrow 5½ to 6½ inches

reddish-brown crown, back and spots

dark central chest spot

long-rounded tail

white breast and throat

from late winter to early summer. It has a clear, sweet song, two or three whistles followed by a flutelike trill. Henry David Thoreau took note of the song sparrow's sprightly melody and penned his description of the way it sounded to him: "Maids! Maids! Maids! Hang up your tea-kettle-ettle-ettle."

This bird has a vast range. It is resident year-round in most of the United States, including coastal Alaska, and migrates in the summer into the northern Midwest and north into the Canadian provinces. Wintering populations can be found from the Gulf Coast states into Mexico.

Across this territory, scientists have distinguished thirty different geographical races of song sparrows, varying slightly in size and overall color and also to some extent in the tone and phrases of their songs. Your basic song sparrow is dark brown above and white streaked with brown below, but some of the races are grayish or rusty. All adults, however, have a mark that is easy to see and identifies them with certainty as song sparrows. Smack in the middle of their chests is a large brown spot.

A large number of different habitats will support song sparrows. They live in woodlands, windbreaks, parks, farmlands, and even on beaches. They seem to favor edge habitat, such as clearings in woodlands and brush bordering lawns and pastures.

Song sparrows feed mostly on seeds from many weeds, grasses, and grains, but they also eat insects. If you want to attract song sparrows, let crabgrass and dandelions grow on your lawn, because the seeds of both are among their common foods. Although they do not generally use feeders, song sparrows will take millet and sunflower from the ground. Water draws song sparrows like a magnet. They are most abundant in cover along streams, ponds, and wetlands, but putting out even a small water source will appeal to them.

Song sparrows will nest in yards with appropriate cover because a breeding pair requires little in the way of territory compared to many other birds—no more than an acre and a half and often much less. They usually nest on or very near the ground. Their well-hidden nests are constructed of materials such as grasses, weeds, and leaves. Usually the song sparrow lays between four and six eggs.

common grackle,
11 to 13 inches
yellow eye
deep bronze or dull purple on back
iridescent purple on head
wedge-shaped tail

Common Grackle

As far as its relationship with humans goes, the common grackle is a Dr. Jekyll and Mr. Hyde. Common grackles are ravagers of insects. A flock of grackles will descend on a lawn or plowed field and sweep it clean of insect pests such as grubs, caterpillars, and grasshoppers. However, grackles, being omnivorous, also ravage agricultural crops such as grain. The agricultural damage that grackles do is caused not only by their voracious appetites but because they are highly social creatures that often travel in large, even immense, flocks that can contain thousands of birds. Common grackles form huge roosts, especially during the winter, when they may mix with starlings and other blackbirds, grackles actually being blackbirds themselves. The number of birds in some of these roosts has been estimated in the millions. The presence of so many birds in one place can create health and sanitation problems as their droppings pile up on the ground and coat trees, buildings, and automobiles.

Common grackles nest from the East Coast west to Texas and central British Columbia. Aggressive and highly adaptable, they utilize a large variety of habitats that range from farmlands and open woodlands to suburbs and cities. Smaller flocks of grackles will drop by suburban yards to forage on lawns. Feeders attract them. Even though they are large birds they will attempt to perch on tube feeders—but seldom with much success. Sunflower or corn scattered on the ground or in a platform feeder is best if you want grackles.

Despite their bad habits, common grackles are indisputably handsome and interesting birds. Seen in sunlight, their black plumage shines like metal. Common grackles along the Atlantic coast north to southern New England have a purple cast to their plumage, while those in the rest of the country have a bronzy sheen. Grackles under a feeder, especially during breeding season, often perform highly ritualized displays, strutting in front of one another with beaks pointed toward the sky and yellow eyes gleaming.

Two other grackles also inhabit North America. Both are named after their spectacular tails. The great-tailed grackle of the southern plains and Southwest is quite large, up to eighteen inches long, about half of that length being tail. The slightly smaller boat-tailed grackle, which lives along the coast from the Middle Atlantic states to Texas, closely resembles it.

Common grackles nest in small colonies of two dozen or so nests spread out through trees, shrubs, and bushes. The nest appears sloppily built of weeds, sticks, and grasses plastered together with mud. Grackles living near the ocean often incorporate seaweed into their nests. Grackles lay between four and seven eggs, which produce clamorous young. Each spring, several pairs of grackles nest in the huge Norway spruce behind my home, and once the young hatch, the backyard resounds from dawn to dusk with their squalling demands for food.

Northern Flicker

There are two races of the northern flicker that vary in certain markings from one another: the red-shafted and yellow-shafted. Both races get their names from the color of feathers under their wings and tails: golden-yellow on the yellow-shafted and salmon-red on the red-shafted. These colors flash during flight but cannot be seen when the bird is in a tree or on the ground. However, there are other differences in markings that are more obvious. The yellow-shafted has a red patch, similar to that of many

gray

northern flicker
13 inches

red crescent on nape,
black bib on chest

brown back
and wings with
black bars

golden-yellow
or salmon
under wings

white rump

tan

male has
black mustache

tan
spotted
belly

other woodpeckers, on the nape of its neck; the red-shafted doesn't. The male yellow-shafted has a black mark behind its bill resembling a mustache, while the male red-shafted's mustache is red. For a while, taxonomists considered the two flickers as distinct species, but they have since changed their minds. Perhaps the two flickers are one species in the process of diverging and the distinctive markings of each are adaptations with some sort of survival value that relates to where each lives.

Most red-shafted flickers are western birds; yellow-shafted birds are eastern. In some areas, the two forms hybridize. The ability of both flickers to inhabit almost all of North America shows that they are very adaptable. Like the American robin and the barn swallow, flickers range the continent south of the Arctic tree line. Northern birds edge south in the winter, but in most of the United States flickers can be seen year-round. Flickers are seldom city birds, but most other habitats where trees grow, even if the trees are widely scattered, are home to them.

For a woodpecker, the northern flicker is rather an odd duck. Your average woodpecker searches for food on trees, where it finds insects such as grubs and beetles. Flickers gorge on ants that they usually locate on the ground, which is the reason they are often seen probing lawns. While ants are the flicker's main source of sustenance, it also consumes many other foods, both animals and plants. Among the other insects eaten by flickers are beetles, crickets, and grasshoppers. The flicker's primary plant food is berries, so plantings such as serviceberry, blackberry, elderberry, and winterberries will interest them. Berries and, to a degree, seeds are especially important to flickers during the winter, when the availability of animal foods declines. Lacking animal prey, they will readily come to suet feeders during the cold months.

Flickers nest in a hole that they dig in a tree, and sometimes in buildings or utility poles, and often make use of nest boxes, if these are offered. Although sometimes the flicker nest is close to the ground, this bird usually prefers penthouse living and often digs its holes as high as sixty feet up. A female may lay as many as nine eggs.

Cedar Waxwing

Lucky are those who have cedar waxwings in their yard. Cedar waxwings and their close cousins, Bohemian wax-

cedar waxwing 7 to 8 inches

black mask

warm brown crest and back, yellow belly

gray tail and wings

red tips on secondary wing feathers

white under tail and wings

yellow band

wings, rate among the most beauteous of North American songbirds. Their plumage is not only colorful, it is so sleek it looks polished. Unfortunately, I have only seen them in and around my town a few times in almost thirty years. This may be partly due to the fact that cedar waxwings can be difficult to see because they often stay among thick foliage high in trees. However, it also may be due to the fact that they are restless vagabonds that never seem to settle down in one particular area for long. They may stay around a place for a few months and then head out for another feeding ground. Sometimes, they will breed in a locality for several seasons but then not be seen there for a year or more.

Range maps indicate that cedar waxwings breed across the northern United States and Canada, that they are present in the southern portion of their breeding range in all seasons, and that they will be found in the remainder of the country during the winter. Because of their wandering ways, however, cedar waxwings cannot always be counted on to be where the books say they are.

Bohemian waxwings are the more northerly of the two species, nesting from central Canada through Alaska and wintering in the western United States and southern Canada. They are birds of the boreal forest, while cedar waxwings live in country that has either coniferous or deciduous trees as well as in open areas. Bohemian waxwings also move about erratically. In both cases, the northern movements of waxwings seem to be dictated by the presence or absence of the berries that they heavily depend upon for food.

Berry bushes and vines, as well as trees that bear fruit such as cherries, may draw waxwings to your yard—if they happen to be around. Mention was made earlier about birds that occasionally get drunk on fermenting fruit. Cedar waxwings are apparently heavy hitters, because they seem to imbibe more than most.

Waxwings get their name from the way that the secondary feathers of the male are tipped with red that looks as glossy as fingernails painted with nail polish. The body of the cedar waxwing is brown on the head, wings, and shoulders and grayish on the rump and back, while the Bohemian waxwing is a basic gray. The hues that make them so colorful are confined to small areas but complement their muted body plumage the way accessories do a tasteful suit or dress. In addition to their red-tipped secondaries, waxwings have a black mask and a band of yellow across the tip of their tails. The wings of the Bohemian waxwing are daubed with white and yellow as well as red.

Bohemian waxwings build their nests on horizontal branches of evergreen trees, usually near the trunk. Cedar waxwings make use of various types of trees as nest sites. They often lay up to half a dozen eggs.

Hermit Thrush

The hermit thrush is found in forests of conifers, of deciduous trees, or of both. As its name implies, the hermit thrush is a secretive bird that likes to stay hidden. It stays mostly on or near to the ground and has a preference for thickets. A formal backyard is unlikely to attract hermit thrushes, but if your property has some low-growing tangles—and,

hermit thrush
6 to 7 inches

↑ rusty-reddish tail

↑ thin eyering

tends to flit wings and bob tail when perched

belly spots

better yet, if there is a woodland or wooded park nearby—
this graceful bird may be enticed into an occasional visit.
Even if you do not see them, hermit thrushes are wonderful
to have around when they are in song. Their clear music is
often described in terms such as "flutelike," but descriptions such as this do it an injustice. The sweet, musical song
of the hermit thrush is a paean to nature, and if it really
does resemble the notes of a flute, then the person playing
the instrument must be Pan.

The hermit thrush is well camouflaged for a life spent
mostly on the ground. It is grayish brown above and white
below, with dark spots on its breast. Most of the hermit
thrush's breeding range is shared by the wood thrush,
which it closely resembles. One way to tell the difference
between them is to look at the tail, which in the hermit
thrush has a distinctly rusty cast. Another way is to look at
the spots on the underparts. Those on the wood thrush are
more pronounced and extend beyond the breast to the
belly.

Hermit thrushes nest throughout the western mountain
states, up into Canada and Alaska, and in a broad north-
easterly swath to New England and south to Maryland. A
few stay in the southern portions of their nesting range for
the winter. However, most head for the southern states and
beyond, as far as Central America. Insects, spiders, and
other small invertebrates constitute the major portion of
the hermit thrush's diet, but it eats berries as well.

The nest that the hermit thrush builds, on the ground
or only a few feet above it, looks delicate but is of strong
construction. The building materials include the finer stuff
of the woodland floor—pine needles, mosses, and even
ferns. These, along with twigs and grasses, are crafted into

a sturdy cup where three to six eggs are deposited by the female.

house sparrow
5½ to 6 inches
brown nape
wings black and brown streaked with white wing bar
gray head cap and breast, black bib on male only

House Sparrow

The house sparrow is a foreign import and does not belong to the same family as American sparrows. The group of birds to which house sparrows belong is variously described as "weaver finches," "Old World sparrows," or "weaver birds." This is a large group of birds, consisting of more than 250 different species that are native to Eurasia, Africa, and Australia. Scientists have different opinions about the relationships of the birds within this group, but suffice to say that weavers have a real presence upon the global avian scene. Most weavers are very social birds that live in large flocks, and many nest in colonies. Several species of weavers build large nests that are carefully woven out of vegetation and may house hundreds of birds. The nests of others, such as the house sparrows, are of slovenly construction, little more than a jumble of sticks, grasses, and weeds.

House sparrows are native to Eurasia and Africa, but they now range over all of North America south of the Arctic tundra. Along with feral pigeons, they thrive both in the country and in the hearts of our largest cities, although scientists believe they are declining in some areas. They place their nests virtually anywhere they can jam them, including on building ledges, under bridges, in nest boxes, in tree cavities, and sometimes even in mailboxes and atop streetlights. If a nesting site is large enough, several pairs of house sparrows may build their nests there in close proximity to one another.

As a rule, birders dislike house sparrows with a fierce passion because they outcompete native species, especially bluebirds, for nesting sites. However, house sparrows deserve a place on this listing of excellent backyard birds because of their ability to live and breed in cities. They bring avian sights and sounds—a flock can be exceedingly noisy—into urban areas where few other birds can survive. A feeder with almost any type of seed will attract house sparrows almost immediately—if you want them.

If you take the time to watch them, house sparrows can be intriguing. They always seem to be busy eating, building nests, or quarreling. During the breeding season, male house sparrows brawl with one another furiously. These battles involve nonviolent displays such as crouching with wings outspread and head bobbing. Unlike most other birds, however, male house sparrows often take off the gloves and viciously peck one another.

Once paired off, the male and female house sparrow cooperate in building their nest. Surprisingly, since the nest appears to be a sloppy affair, they may take almost a week to complete it. Often, castoffs such as bits of string and cloth are used along with natural matter as building materials.

Although house sparrows in search of a nest site will sometimes kill the nestlings and even adults of other species, they do not tolerate any bird that tries to interfere with their own parental responsibilities. The male is especially protective and will aggressively assault other birds that come near the nest. House sparrows lay between three and seven eggs, but generally there are four eggs to a clutch.

In and around St. Louis, Missouri, lives a Eurasian relative of the house sparrow that, like it, is an introduced species. The Eurasian (or "European") tree sparrow resembles the house sparrow in appearance but not in disposition. It is a far gentler bird than the feisty house sparrow and, although it does inhabit some urban parks, is more a rural and suburban bird than one of the city.

Sharp-Shinned Hawk

Relentless pursuer of small birds, the sharp-shinned hawk is a common bird of prey throughout much of North America—and it doesn't hesitate to include feeding stations among its favorite hunting grounds. During the

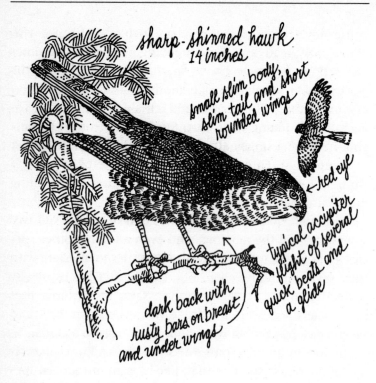

sharp-shinned hawk
14 inches

small slim body,
slim tail and short
rounded wings

←red eye

typical accipiter
flight of several
quick beats and
a glide

dark back with
rusty bars on breast
and under wings

breeding season, it lives as far north as the Arctic tree line; in fact, the bulk of the continent's sharp-shinned population nest in the boreal forest. The approach of winter sends Alaskan and Canadian birds south. Many sharp-shinned hawks from the lower forty-eight states migrate southward as well, some as far as Central America, but others remain for the winter, when they are particularly attracted to concentrations of songbirds around feeders.

Sharp-shinned hawks are well known for their mass migrations. During spring and fall, they travel over specific migration routes, often following mountain ridges and coastlines. These areas produce frequent updrafts of air that make soaring easier for the hawks, thereby cutting down on their energy expenditure. In a single season, thousands of sharp-shinned hawks may funnel through an area where the topography below creates prime migratory conditions. Sometimes they pass overhead individually, one after another, every few minutes. At other times, several hawks can be seen together overhead; however, they do not travel in organized flocks.

Sharp-shinned hawks are seldom found in areas without trees, nevertheless, they prefer open woodland and bushy areas to dense forest. These more open habitats usually have a greater variety of small birds, which are the sharp-shinned hawk's bread and butter. Sharp-shinned hawks work hard for their dinner. According to some estimates, only 10 percent of their hunts end successfully.

Bluish gray above and white with rusty streaks on its underparts, the sharp-shinned is about a foot in length, which makes it only slightly larger than some of the birds upon which it preys. It prefers conifers as sites for its nest, which is a shallow construction of twigs and sticks. Although sharp-shinned hawks have been known to lay up to eight eggs, the usual number is about half of that.

Eastern Screech Owl

Wooded areas are the home of the eastern screech owl and its counterpart, the western screech owl. Both frequently turn up in suburban backyards and city parks with sizable trees. Since it is nocturnal, the eastern screech owl is seldom seen (sometimes it can be observed by day while

eastern screech owl - 8 to 9 inches

young may not have ear tufts

yellow eyes

bill usually light

white spots on wings

two varieties: rust and gray; western species is brown

roosting deep within the boughs of a tree), but its presence is often announced by its eerie calls. To people unfamiliar with the calls made by a screech owl, the sounds it sends echoing through the night can be downright scary. The eastern owl typically utters a trembling whistle, rising and falling in pitch. The western's primary call is a series of short whistles, given with increasing speed. Both owls also produce series of yelping notes.

Both screech owls are considered "eared owls"—that is, they have feathered ear tufts. They are small creatures, only about eight or nine inches long. The eastern screech owl has gray and red phases; the western bird is brown.

Screech owls are not picky about food as long as it is animal protein. They hunt small worms and other invertebrates, fish, amphibians, reptiles, and small mammals, especially mice. Songbirds, often taken unawares as they awaken just before dawn, are also included among the owls' prey. Songbirds that screech owls are known to prey upon are eastern phoebes, cedar waxwings, American robins, and catbirds. However, since screech owls have such a varied diet, their predation upon songbirds is not nearly as heavy as that of the sharp-shinned hawk. Screech owls have an astonishing repertoire of hunting techniques. Their usual plan of attack is to wing silently through the air, watching the ground below for victims. Screech owls also have been reported walking on the ground and entering the water in search of prey. Sometimes they strike insects from a perch on a branch.

Usually, the female screech owl incubates the eggs while the male brings back the results of the hunt. After the young hatch—generally four or five of them—both parents hunt overtime to meet their demands for food, sometimes making dozens, even scores, of trips in a night. They nest in tree cavities, abandoned woodpecker holes, and nest boxes.

Appendix A:

HOW TO MAKE A BACKYARD BIRD JOURNAL

Write It Down Now

You can increase your enjoyment of backyard birding by keeping a backyard bird journal. A journal can contain notations about the types of birds that visit your yard, when they appear, and what they do there. Having a record of the different birds that visit your yard can be very rewarding. Besides words, your journal can contain sketches of what you see. Looking over your notes from the past may help you anticipate when different kinds of birds are likely to turn up in the future. You can also compare behavior of the same species at different times of the day or season, or contrast the behavior of different species. Write down the details of what you have seen as soon as possible after making your observations. And don't put it on a scrap of paper with the idea that you will transfer it to your journal later. You may well lose the scrap or forget about it. As a journalist and naturalist, I have been trained to keep accurate, permanent notes. Even so, there have been times when, while engaged in an activity other than bird-watching, I happened to notice an interesting avian vignette but felt I was too busy to pull out a journal and jot it down. Instead, my observation was hastily scrawled on the nearest piece of paper available—the back of a used envelope, for example. All too often, my observations have been lost in the wastepaper basket. The best idea is to keep your journal and writing instrument in the room in your house where you most often see birds and carry it with you if you go outside to watch them.

Pen and Paper

The notebook containing your journal of observations should be small enough to be portable and large enough for you to write legibly in and, if you choose, include drawings. A good paper size is six by nine inches. Pages should be enclosed in a loose-leaf binder because that makes it easier for you to rearrange or insert new sheets of notes. As for a writing instrument, a pencil is not recommended. Sure, you can erase penciled notes, but they are not as long-lasting as those written in ink. Purists, especially those who include drawings in their journal, use fine-pointed fountain pens with India ink, but any pen with a hard point will do.

Organizing a Journal

Your journal is not a diary but a record of observations that should have a uniform format. For a backyard birder, the two best formats are to organize entries according to either species or dates. At the top of each page, write down either the species or the date. Don't end one entry and start another on the same page. This may save paper, but it makes individual observations difficult to find at a later date.

When making notes, you don't have to please your high school English teacher by writing eloquent prose. Be telegraphic and write down the pertinent facts and words. Still, try to be as comprehensive as you can. If a cardinal is calling, for example, try to identify the vegetation in which it is perched. If you can, write down the outside temperature and other weather conditions. The following are suggested formats and samples of the observations that you may want to include in your journal. They are not written in stone. Adapt them to your needs.

Organizing by Species

HOUSE FINCH

DATE: May 27, 1997

TIME OF DAY: 9 A.M.

WEATHER: Sunny, temperature about 55 degrees F.

PLACE: Nest on lamp above front door

OBSERVATION: Young house finches calling for food. Hairy feathers on their head visible. Nestlings very noisy. Can even hear them while I am in the upstairs bathroom, shaving. Mother finch comes to nest. Can't see what she is feeding them but obviously they are eating.

Organizing by Dates

March 2, 1997
Common Grackle

TIME OF DAY: 10 A.M.

WEATHER: In the forties (F), windy and sunny.

OBSERVATION: Heard grackle calls. Large flock, perhaps in the hundreds, settled into trees. Calling so loud it reminds me of Hitchcock's movie *The Birds*. Grackles stay around for about an hour, then move on. First sighting this season. Spring is coming.

Appendix B:

BACKYARD BIRDING PROJECTS

Get Involved Through the Cornell Laboratory of Ornithology Citizen-Science Projects

The Laboratory of Ornithology at Cornell University is a membership institute to which many birders belong. Members receive publications and discounts at the laboratory's birding shop. The laboratory also conducts scientific citizen-science projects that depend upon the help of birders. Following are descriptions of two projects in which backyard birders are involved. A small fee is charged to participate in each. Further information on these projects and on membership can be obtained from the Cornell Laboratory of Ornithology, Program Services, 159 Sapsucker Woods Road, Ithaca, NY 14850, telephone (607) 254-2440. The laboratory's e-mail address is birdeducation@cornell.edu.

Project Feeder Watch

Thousands of backyard birders across North America have turned their hobby into a valuable research tool by taking part in the Cornell Laboratory's Project Feeder Watch. Once every two weeks, from November through March, participants watch birds at feeders, record what they see on forms provided by the laboratory, and send them in for analysis in the spring. The information gathered by feeder watchers helps scientists develop data on subjects such as long-term trends in winter bird populations, features that attract birds, and movements of nomadic species during the winter. Participants receive a bird calendar and a newsletter.

Cornell Nest Box Network

Participants in the Cornell Nest Box Network gather information on cavity-nesting birds and are seeking answers to questions about their nesting and reproductive behavior. Birders monitor nest boxes and the birds that use them with the aid of a research kit provided by the laboratory. The kit includes information on how to build and place nest boxes as well as a newsletter. Information sent to the laboratory by networkers is studied and organized by scientists. Observers can put as much time into the project as they wish.

INDEX

Page numbers in italics indicate illustrations